ACKNOWLEDGEMENTS

There were so many people who made immense contributions to OUR story that it is virtually impossible to name them all here. Rather I have decided to identify four groups of people; any individual could be considered a member of any one or all of these groups.

The hard-working American: This nation is a wonderful place to live. What we experienced in OUR travels was the fruits of great vision and hard labor that brought great ideas to realization. Every great building - from the Empire State building in New York to the Sears tower in Chicago to the TransAmerica building in San Francisco and all of those in between, including other massive city skyscrapers to smaller apartment complexes, single family homes, and the restored pioneer cabins of the old west—is the result of someone's vision and the labor of many. The same goes for the man-made monuments throughout this country. To name a few, there are: Mt. Rushmore in South Dakota, the Gateway Arch in St. Louis, the Space Needle in Seattle, the Golden Gate Bridge in San Francisco, and the Statue of Liberty in New York. These monuments and all of the others are the result of vision, planning, and labor. The best example of a monument in progress is Crazy Horse near Rapid City, South Dakota. I encourage you to go see this great sculpture and think about the vision, planning, and labor it takes to make it happen. The Eisenhower interstate system and all of the great roads of this nation allowed for safe, efficient and enjoyable travel. As we traveled on these roads and witnessed the man-made wonders of our great nation, I couldn't help but think of all of the sweat it took to make it what it is today. Even more, I felt very proud to be an American. It is the men and women of the past and present that helped build the buildings, create the monuments, raise the bridges, and lay the highways of this great nation who I applaud. I thank the hard-working American for your contributions.

The running community: It has been an absolute privilege to be associated with this group of simply wonderful people. For every volunteer who handed out water and sp~~   ~~ pt us weary runners on course, thar' ame out to cheer us on, thank you. t and other

D1503018

agencies who controlled traffic flow and maintained safe courses, thank you. For those who ensured the port-a-potties were strategically placed, a very special thank you. For all of the race directors and their staffs who worked tirelessly to put on these challenging events, thank you. For the media outlets that advertised and covered the events, thank you. This includes a very special thanks to marathonguide.com whose web site I lived by during this quest. You guys are the best. To my fellow marathoners who I have been so honored to have run these many miles with, thank you. Keep on running! I truly appreciate all of the meaningful contributions from everyone mentioned.

There are three individuals I would like to single out as having the greatest impact in this quest. First is Dean Rademaker who is the original pioneer of the 50 States and DC marathon group. His vision to recognize and acknowledge the individual accomplishment of running a marathon in all 50 states and DC is simply genius. Thank you, Dean, for giving it a beginning. Also thanks to Jerry Schaver who continues to manage the 50 and DC group as director. Finally, it is Steve Boone who took the concept a bit further and started up the 50 States Marathon Club. You rock, Steve. I find it difficult to express the honor I feel being a member of both of these organizations.

Family and friends: Initially I never intended to write a book. I saw myself as the 'absent dad' because I worked nights and lots of extra hours. So this quest was a way to give back some quality time to my immediate family. It was the genuine interest and inquiries about our excursions from my relatives, friends, and co-workers that inspired me to take things a little further than a scrapbook. When we went to Kansas it was simply a scrapbook. Because of my Aunt Mary's enthusiasm when we left Kansas, it became a mission to write a book. So my thanks begin with Aunt Mary. My appreciation continues on to each and every relative who in some way played a role in enriching our lives in this story. Since most of you are characters in the text already, I'll pass on noting individual names here. Thanks to you all for being a part of this story.

Of course the many characters in this story are not limited to relatives. Thank you to all of the friendly faces of our friends who were integral parts of this story. Thank you for being part of OUR LIVES.

Thanks to my friends and co-workers at Continental Airlines who indirectly went along for the ride. Your enthusiastic responses to my stories gave me the added encouragement needed to complete the quest. This is especially true when I neared the end and was experiencing a little bit of 'burn out.' We have a very special team and I am proud to be a part of it.

For my friends at Arbor Books who were instrumental in helping me with this story, especially Fran Reed, I thank you.

Teachers and educators: If you are a teacher or an educator there are times you have experienced the emotion of having a sometimes hopeless and thankless occupation. In most cases it takes years for the fruits of your labors to be realized. In most cases you will never know since it is not a common practice for students to stay in touch with their teachers. The challenges become even greater when dealing with special needs students. You are not placed last here on acknowledgements because that's where I see you on my list of priorities. When I went to school I was taught that most people have a tendency to remember the first and last things on a list the most. Well, I want people to know that teachers come first on my list. My hat's off to the teachers of this nation.

MAP TRANSPORTATION LEGEND

NOTE: Chapter openings indicate distance traveled from author's home in Streamwood, IL to the marathon starting point

 = traveled by car, SUV, or van

 = traveled by plane

 = traveled by train

TABLE OF CONTENTS

To Erin, Austin, and Jeanne:
You all were worth every mile. Thanks for making them special.

Introduction
The Gift

It was small, not much bigger than a book and it came in a colorfully wrapped package with an excessive amount of tape. It was very evident that it would be a struggle to get past the wrapping to see what was inside. There was a note attached advising that the utmost care must be taken when opening because the greatest treasure one could ever have was inside. The note also had a riddle. *"Be not in haste and break what is sealed, for only with time and care will the treasure be revealed. Forcing the package open with hammer or knife will result in the treasure being broken and scarred for life."*

What did this mean? If there was a treasure inside, then I must get it out. Wasn't treasure supposed to be gold and coins? How could I possibly damage those? There was so much tape; I did not have the patience to carefully peel it off. Ignoring the instructions, I used my pocket knife to quickly cut through the tape and wrapping. What I found was a small rectangular wooden box with a frame made of oak and a center of thin plywood. There were some gashes where my knife had penetrated through the plywood, but the box remained intact. Treasure was inside this box, and I was determined to get to it. There simply did not appear to be any way to open it to get inside. Since the instructions stated not to use a hammer or knife, I needed to find another way to open it. I went to the garage and put the box in a vice and proceeded to spin the handle until the wood began to split open. As the first little opening revealed something glistening, my heart began to race. Excited by the knowledge that I was about to be the recipient of a treasure, I wondered how much was in the box.

I spun the handle one more time and, 'pop,' the wood frame snapped and the contents fell to the floor. I looked down and saw the reflection of my scarred face in the shards of a broken and shattered mirror.

Jolted awake, I jumped out of bed and hurried to the bathroom to look into the mirror. The face staring back at me was not scarred or broken but certainly shaken. As I dressed, I wondered if my strange dream had any particular meaning. However, mornings are busy in our household and I needed to get moving. Seven-thirty a.m. is no time to dwell on deeper meanings. I went downstairs, sat at the breakfast table and glanced at the morning paper while my wife Jeanne prepared breakfast. My son Austin, age five, sat at the end of the table on my right and Erin, my two-year-old daughter was in her highchair on my left. It wasn't long before Jeanne joined us and we sat at the table as one happy family. As I finished breakfast, I found myself thinking about my dream and what it could possibly mean.

It was the summer of 1994, and at the time we had been living on Oahu, Hawaii for three years. Initially, I thought the riddle applied to Austin. At five years old, there was something very different about him. He was not yet communicating in full sentences, had problems with motor skills, difficulty socially fitting in with other kids his age and, at times, he was oppositional. We knew something wasn't right, but couldn't figure out exactly why. He certainly was a hard nut to crack. Was he the treasure yet to be revealed?

It would be another seven years of frustration and grief before he was diagnosed with Asperger's syndrome. Asperger's Syndrome (AS) is a neurological disorder most commonly believed to be a high functioning form of Autism. Children with AS process very differently and this creates serious challenges for both the child and for the family. As Erin grew older, she displayed many of the same characteristics as Austin. We spent years beating ourselves up worrying that we were doing something wrong only to discover that the answer was autism. All along I reflected on my dream and reminded myself that our children are two wonderful gifts and that each requires very careful unpackaging to reveal their true treasures within.

That same summer, I decided to take on the challenge of running my first marathon. While initially it was something I wanted to do just to say I did it, my ulterior motives were to stay in shape, set a goal, and live by the example I hoped my kids would someday follow. Strangely enough, I did not even enjoy running, but I do believe that sometimes in life we have to do things that we do not like because there is great value in the end results.

Back then I had no idea that this first marathon would ultimately lead me to take on the challenge of running marathons in each of the fifty states. In addition to allowing me to discover my own strengths, abilities and, perhaps, my own internal treasure, I had hoped that this quest would ultimately benefit Austin and Erin. The experience far exceeded my wildest hopes and expectations! Our travels have allowed us to see so much that our great nation has to offer. We caught up with old family members and made many new friends. The experiences that we went through we will treasure for our lifetime. It was an extraordinarily remarkable experience in which my kids were able to gain a real life education and I believe they learned much that they would not have inside a classroom.

When I began, I never intended to write a book about my experiences. I kept a scrapbook with pictures and souvenirs so that Austin and Erin would have a tangible remembrance of our adventures. Somewhere along the way after much drama, laughter, adversity, sorrow, frustration, excitement, disappointment, pride, and success, I felt compelled to share **OUR** story with others. I hope you enjoy it.

1

A Tough Beginning
December 11, 1994

HAWAII

Six months before the race, I filled out the entry form and paid the fee. That was my first inclination that something was wrong with runners. I mean, shouldn't I be the one getting paid to run 26.2 miles? Regardless of my point of view, it was now official. Still, there were doubts. I didn't really make up my mind 100 percent until the night before. I just kept going with the thought, "I think I'll run."

So much was happening it's amazing I kept any thoughts, but this one was like a bright spot to hold on to. Continental Airlines, for whom I was a load planner, decided it could do without me and about 600 other employees. The sky had fallen. Hawaii is one of the most expensive places in the U.S. to live, but we didn't want to leave the island. Searching for shells on a soft beach below the mountains had become part of our lives, and the people were so friendly. With our Hawaiian shirts and shorts, we were "resident tourists," and it was our mission to visit every tourist site on Oahu. We had visited the Polynesian Cultural Center. There, students from areas around the Pacific, like Tahiti and New Zealand, welcomed us to their sections with music and folk art. It was like a tiny trip to each locale. At the end of the day, we watched boats manned by Hawaiians in native outfits by firelight as island music played.

We had also gone to luaus, climbed Diamond Head Crater, cheered the Pro Bowl football games, and watched surfers at sunrise and sunset. Now it was our island, too. I had to find a new job soon, otherwise we couldn't afford to stay. Fortunately, I was offered one with a hazardous waste company, packing and loading waste for ships to the mainland United States. I also started night school at Hawaii Pacific University to complete a degree in Human Resources Management. I loved going to the classes and parking next to the 'Iolani Palace, where "Hawaii Five–O" was filmed.

All of this meant crowded schedules, with both of us working and caring for the kids, but the important fact was I had work. The new job was so demanding that I stayed physically fit, even if I didn't have much time to actually train. And since Jeanne and I took turns taking care of the kids, they were a workout for me, too. While Jeanne rented cars to passengers at the airport, I'd take care of Austin, 5, and Erin, 2. They could make a trip to the park quite a bit of exercise for Dad. We'd go park hopping, and at each park, I'd take a trash bag and have them clean up before they played. As I had learned on the farms, they were learning that life includes work.

Sunday mornings were special and always started with a breakfast at McDonald's. Every week, they included going to Waikiki beach, the aquarium, the zoo, and then back to Waikiki for ice cream from a local vendor. In the zoo, I always talked to Austin about the animals, repeating their names. "See the kookaburra," or "That's a crocodile." I hoped this would help his learning, but he couldn't remember things well. By the next week, I'd be telling him everything again, as I carried him on my shoulders and pushed Erin in her stroller. I was, indeed, exercising, although I wasn't running, and we were having fun. My plate was full with work, studies and family, but I always held onto my plan to run the marathon.

I read a little about marathons and learned that the first one was run by an Athenian courier called Pheidippides in 490 B.C. He ran from the town of Marathon to Athens to tell the Athenians that they had won the Battle of Marathon. The trip was 22 miles. It was such a famous run that a "marathon" of 40 kilometers, or 24.8 miles, was included in the first Greek Olympics in 1896. The International Olympic Committee standardized the distance at 26 miles for the 1908 Olympic Games in London. So why the "point two" more miles? That was added on at Queen Alexandra's insistence, so that the race finished in front of the royal box at the Olympic Stadium in White City. So when that last "point two" miles seems too much, thank the queen. Since then, all marathons have been that distance: Twenty–six point two long, long miles, on sand, roads, up and down hills, whatever the local terrain included, as well as people; hundreds of people in the races, and hundreds more, watching. If you did well, they saw. If you didn't, they also saw. But I would be running at my own pace, against my own time. I thought if I could just complete it at all, I'd be proud.

Sometimes running was all pushed to the side as we struggled to understand the challenges our children presented. Austin was not yet making full sentences. We read all the Dr. Seuss books to him, worked on his ABCs, giving him what help we could with his kindergarten work, but something wasn't right. We kept telling the doctors and his teachers, but they were little help. (It wasn't until he was 12 that we finally found out he has Asperger's Syndrome, a condition in which children have inappropriate, or one–sided, interactions and poor nonverbal communication, among other traits.) With Erin, we knew from the beginning that something was wrong. Her feet were very swollen. She was tested right away, and we were told she had Turner Syndrome and that she was missing an "X" of one of her chromosomes, but we didn't fully understand all the implications for a long time. We just knew we had two children we would dote on and shower with love, and work full time, or more, to support. And beyond that, I'd stay in shape with my running. So finally, the night before the 1994 marathon, I committed myself to entering. I also assured myself that whatever I did, I would reach the finish line. For this first one, Jeanne and the kids were not there to cheer me on, but she wished me well as I left the house in the pre–dawn darkness.

Running is big in Hawaii. Almost every weekend there's a race in Hawaii. But this was THE race, the *marathon*. The furthest I had run in training was fourteen miles, a little over half the distance. I didn't even know if I could make it the whole way, but I was there to give it my all. For me, and most runners, running is not about finishing first. It is a personal thing. It is an activity by which we gauge our health. It is not about competing with others, but rather of setting personal records. It's about keeping one's weight down, breathing right, feeling strong inside, and the exhilaration of accomplishment. In spite of all these pluses, I simply don't like it. It's work. It's an inconvenience. It's training in the rain and cold. It's suffering through injuries, blistered feet, runner's toe, shin splints, sore knees, sore muscles, and an aching back. I've experienced all of that. It all sucks. Why did I decide to do it? Responsibility. I've been given the privilege of a healthy body, and it's my responsibility to myself and to my family to maintain good health. I also hoped that over the years my kids would see and follow this example in their own ways, maintaining their own fitness. I wanted to lead by example.

The run started at 5a.m., when it was still cool, if there is such a thing in Hawaii. The field was massive. There were over 25,000 runners. I worked my way to the middle and waited. I was very nervous and uncertain, despite the festive environment. There was an assortment of feelings racing through my mind, good and not good, all at the same time.

Then the countdown began. I held my breath. Bang! The gun put my feet in motion, and I was actually running a marathon. But so were thousands of others. It was so crowded it took me over five minutes just to reach the start line, and another half mile before I could get my pace.

Once the crowd spread out, I was able to run and look at where I was, wonderful Hawaii. I loved running through downtown Honolulu and through Waikiki. There were thousands of spectators. I relaxed and started to enjoy the run. It felt great. I was actually doing well. I sensed the warmth and welcome light of the sun rising behind me.

Then, at mile 15, my right calf gave me a spasm. I thought it was weird. It's the feeling you get right before your muscle has a charley horse late at night that wakes you screaming. I stopped and stretched. I tried to keep going. It happened again. My lower leg was turning to spaghetti. It happened several times over the next mile. I'd stop and stretch and try to keep going. Around mile 16 it happened to my left leg, too. The rest of my body felt fine, but my legs were falling apart. I forced myself to keep going despite these strange sensations.

The frequency of the spasms increased. At mile 19, I accepted that I had to walk or I was going to get a terrible leg cramp. I walked from mile 19 to mile 25. It was very disappointing to watch the time tick away. Mile 24 was in a residential area. People were in their yards cheering us on. One guy had several beer kegs in his yard, passing drinks out to the runners. I'm not a beer drinker, but I took one, and it was the best beer I had tasted in my life. It was a hot and humid day, and I was drained. The coldness felt good going down.

Mile 25 was a on a hill that inclined around the base of the Diamond Head crater. The ocean was on the left. The finish was getting close. At the top of the hill, I started to trot again. I slowly worked my way down, running the last mile. At last, I reached the long–awaited finish line and ran over it. I had completed my first marathon! I was sore, but I had made it. Walking six miles had saved my legs from being even more sore. I looked around at the crowd; people congratulating runners, runners smiling, runners grimacing, and runners resting. That's when I really missed Jeanne. I took the first bus to the airport and walked up to the Budget rental desk, where she was working, proudly sporting my finisher's T-shirt. I acted as if it was no big deal and told her my finishing time. How little did we know that this was not the finish, but rather the beginning.

Time: 4:32:05

2

Can I Break Four Hours?
October 11, 1998

When it was time to graduate, I couldn't go to the ceremony because I had a job interview. I had hoped we could stay in Hawaii, but the work offered was in Chicago, so that's where we headed. It was with Continental Airlines in a managerial position. I was back with my airline. We would brave the cold and discover a new world.

We actually moved to a suburb near a forest preserve, so it wasn't Hawaii, but it had its own dark green beauty, and we'd have the colored leaves in the fall. After we settled in, and Jeanne had a job, too, I took all the overtime I could to chop into the debt we had brought with us. Working 60 to 70 hours a week, plus going to Air Force Reserves once a month, was tough. She worked days and I worked nights, so we barely saw each other. I wasn't there for the kids when they came home from school, and Austin was having more and more trouble with school. Just thinking about missing the chance to help him really tugged at my mind and heart. I focused on going to work and picking up as many hours as I could, because at the time it was, "the right thing to do." That was the motto I created for myself to keep myself on the straight and narrow during times it would have been so much easier to go astray.

Despite our tiring schedules, we still made time to be local tourists, as we did in Hawaii. We took Austin and Erin to see the dinosaur bones in the Museum of Natural History and to visit the Museum of Holography. We also cheered on the Cubs and the White Sox. We were becoming part of the city. One time, Jeanne submitted Austin's name to be the celebrity bat kid at a Chicago Cubs baseball game. I received the phone call, and at first was a little harsh with the lady on the other end. I thought it was another one of those annoying calls from a salesperson. My tune changed when I learned that Austin had been picked. It was a very special day at the ball park. Austin got to sit in the dugout with the players. He got some big name autographs, including Sammy Sosa, Joe Carter, Mark Prior and Ron Santo. His name was announced and put up on the scoreboard. To top things off, the Cubs won five to nothing that day!

I had run two other Honolulu marathons after that first one and was never able to break four hours for the 26.2 miles. When I heard of the Chicago Marathon, I thought maybe this would be the place to do it. The run would be in October, and I decided after we'd been there over a year that I'd give it a try. If I could break four hours, then I would quit running and take up some other form of fitness.

Actually, I hate running. My training for the marathons is terrible. I have no consistency. I never run the required miles to be fit enough to have a good finish. I always have too many conflicts—work, school, family, weather, or even, just plain laziness—to establish a routine running schedule. I spend two weeks training and then I won't run for a month or two. It's really hard to start over again and again. Each time I'm all winded and slower. Sometimes I wonder why I keep punishing myself by doing this.

For Chicago, even hoping to break four hours, I didn't change my training habits. I did enjoy the fitness expo prior to the marathon, however. I bought a Gore–Tex running suit for $200. The idea was to have something to wear while training in Chicago's adverse weather.

With what running I did manage, ready or not, the day arrived. Jeanne and I left the kids with a babysitter and took the Metra to downtown early in the morning. There were thousands of people, but we were sure we could meet afterward. We had agreed upon a place.

During my previous three marathons I learned I didn't hydrate myself enough. You're supposed to start hydration days before a run. Even though it was now only hours beforehand, I was going to hydrate as much as I could, albeit late. I figured I would be better prepared than before. The result was that just before the race, I found myself waiting in the porta–potty line. I made it just in time. Wow! What a relief! Then I lost myself in the masses of other runners waiting for the starting gun. The cold made me want to start, just to get warmer.

The Run

The gun went off, and I was on my way. It took two minutes just to get to the starting line. The first mile was so crowded that it took eleven minutes to complete.

Then I actually began to enjoy myself. Running in Chicago was neat, with so many people cheering me on. I heard people shout out my number many times: "Way to go Number 8,642!" "Keep it up, 8,642!"

There were very few gaps between the spectators. Early on I was looking for one. I was just a tad bit over–hydrated. Fortunately, at about the 1.5 mile mark, I found a gap that had some bushes. There were other runners who were fond of this area, too. We all ensured that the vegetation was well watered. I had a little feeling of déjà vu. It seemed like it was only 15 minutes earlier that I went through similar motions. Wow! What's going on here? At mile 6, I had to go again. Lucky me! Another gap with bushes and more concerned runners just like me. Yes, we were worried that the vegetation might dehydrate just watching us, so we all hosed the green stuff down. My pace was pretty good, considering the slow start and the two quick diversions. Then, suddenly, somewhere just past the halfway point, in the Chinatown area, I started feeling a little rumbling in my tummy. I was going to need to make another stop. A gap with bushes wasn't the correct answer for this nature call. This discomfort slowed me down for a while until I finally saw a mom and pop style Chinese restaurant. When I came out, I was a new man.

As I continued, I was able to maintain a pretty good pace. My legs did get sore and tight during the last few miles, but I kept going. I was going to make it. When I finally crossed the finish line, I had made it in 3 hours, 45 minutes and 44 seconds. *I had broken four hours!* It was a great feeling, and the fatigue and sore legs were forgotten. I had set my goal and made it. Now I wanted to find Jeanne, but the finish area was packed. Everyone was looking for someone for a hug or congratulations. It took 45 minutes for me to find Jeanne. It was great to have her there. We spent the rest of the day walking around Chicago, sightseeing, and we ate lunch at Michael Jordan's restaurant. The Chicago Marathon was a great experience. Even though I had met my goal of under four hours, I felt a need to vindicate myself of those terrible four hour–plus finishes in Hawaii. The question was, could I do it?

Time: 3:45:44

3

Vindicating Myself
December 13, 1998

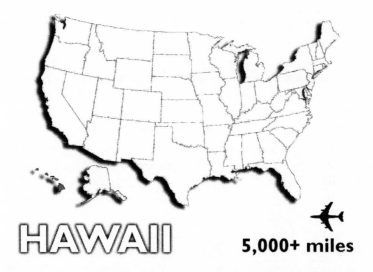

HAWAII

5,000+ miles

I obtained an industry pass on another airline, so I'd have a direct flight from Chicago to Honolulu. It was a short trip, just two days, with about two hours of sleep in the 48. My first step was to head to the beach, where I collected the hollowed–out shells of crabs. I remembered being there with Jeanne, announcing my desire to run the first time. Now, her good wishes were with me as I canvassed the rock ledges and took in the sweet smells of my island. Just beyond my searching, the waves were running their own marathon, rushing to the shore.

There was also time to see old friends and catch up on their lives as they heard of mine. Work and family were going well. Our main concern was dealing with the struggles of Austin in school. Someone, someday, would have to be able to help us. Meanwhile, I'd enjoy this break and put all my energy into running.

The Run

Chicago and Honolulu are enormously popular runs. Both have over 20,000 participants. Runners are supposed to line up in the order of estimated finish time. I went as close to the front as possible. I knew I couldn't finish in two and a half hours, but I wasn't going to lose time working through the crowd, either.

The countdown started. The gun went off, and I was on my way once again in Hawaii. This time, I felt less nervous. I was just happy to be there. It was the same familiar route, with thousands of spectators to cheer runners on. Again, I was running in the pre–dawn glow of the streetlights, since the race began at 5 a.m.

I had an excellent first half. It took an hour and forty minutes. Because of a turnaround point, at miles 9 through 11 the runners on this course passed the runners who were already at miles 15 through 18. I kept going at my steady pace, and as I watched the others, I remembered how many Japanese entrants there were. One of them passed me when I was on mile 18 and he was on mile 10. I heard a "clop, clop, clop" sound, and looked closer. He was wearing wooden platform shoes about five inches high! How could someone possibly run in wooden shoes?

But soon after, I forgot the shoes as my pain arrived. My muscles were tight and sore. I had to slow down in the second half. I even had to walk in parts. By the last three miles, my thighs burned terribly. I was glad to see the same man with beer on his lawn for us at mile 24.

I chugged up Diamond Head Hill, proud that I had not stopped on the hill this time. The finish line in Kapiolani Park was a wonderful sight, and my time was just what I wanted. I had finally gone under four hours in Hawaii. I went straight to a pay phone and called Jeanne. By long distance we shared what was, up until now, one of the most gratifying moments of my life. I just wished she were there, but I knew we would return together to Hawaii someday. I just didn't know when.

I also knew that *if* I ran again, Jeanne would be there, with the kids. No, not if. I *would* run again. Now, where would the next marathon be?

Time: 3:42:58

4

There's A Club For This?
January 17, 1999

TEXAS   **1,167 miles**

I knew we were in Texas when I saw the boots and cowboy hats on the airport passengers and the ceramic longhorn cattle in the gift shops. For this marathon, I decided to make it a family affair. As a family, we hadn't traveled anywhere on a plane together since we left Hawaii for Chicago 18 months ago. Neither Jeanne nor I had collected enough vacation time before. What little time I did have, I had used for the Reserves, so now was our time to go. We had the travel itch, and Houston was ready with a marathon. I could also see other coworkers who had transferred from Hawaii. However, because of time constraints, I could allow only two days. If I were to ever bring them on a future marathon, I knew I'd want at least a day before and another afterward to sightsee and relax, with the day of anxious waiting at the start line squeezed in the middle. That was just a thought, because this was going to be my last race, I reminded myself. I gave another quick glance at the gift shop windows, with Lone Star flags and Texas pralines candy, as I led my group to the curb.

Outside was where I made my mistake. How could an airport be so far away? Had I only known, we would have taken a shuttle bus, but innocently, I hailed a taxi. *Fifty dollars!* This was for a ride from an airport in nowhere to the tall buildings of the actual city. I held my breath as I watched the meter rise faster than my minutes in the marathon. I wanted to point out tourist sights along the way, but I didn't see any. Mostly, I saw numbers rising. Finally, we were delivered to our hotel, and the kids, tired of sitting in planes and taxis, were glad to just be out anywhere. We took them to the pool for a chance to cool off, and then I was glad to get some sleep for tomorrow's race. The next morning, I took a taxi to the start area—a much shorter trip. I had plenty of time to stretch and get ready. It was a pretty good size field. 4,352 runners finished. While waiting for the run to start, I met this group of runners who were planning to enter a marathon in _every_ _state_. I never imagined there were marathons in *each* state. Were they gluttons for punishment or on to something fun?

"This is my fourteenth," one man announced.

Another proudly told me, "I've already run 25."

As I listened, I thought, "That's a neat idea." They had a club for themselves, the people who were running in all 50. Actually, there were two clubs, I was told. Both had internet sites that kept track of the participants' progress and listed the finishers. Cool! This was something I wanted to be a part of. I questioned them about joining and learned I'd have to run seven more after this one to join. Hmm. I had planned this to be my last, but now hearing of this group, maybe I'd give it a try. It would be exciting to be part of a special club like this, and it would be great for the kids, but I wasn't sure I could do it. If I could, and if I planned more time on our trips, they would learn something from each state, and we'd all have a good time. Something to think about. But first I had to run this one.

The Run

The first mile surprised me. I did it in 6 minutes and 50 seconds. I thought right away that I would be able to set a personal record (PR), but being Houston, it was humid out. I was sweating quite a bit and the heat was taking a lot out of me. During the middle miles, around 14 and 15, my legs began to get tight. I had a personal goal of running the entire distance without stopping. By the time I reached 19 miles, I was hurting. I really wanted to walk some at that point. I kept going one mile at a time. Even though my pace had slowed down, I was still looking at a sub four–hour finish. They had planned the route through some nice parks, and the downtown section had thousands of cheering supporters. I was enjoying the trip. Yes, maybe I could actually run 50 plus the D.C. race. As I ran, I visualized the fun I would have. It was a realistic goal. However, by mile 22, my legs were terribly sore. They hurt something fierce. I hadn't stopped yet. I would try another mile. Just past the 23 mile mark, there was a small incline. My legs hurt so bad I just couldn't make it. Maybe this *should* be my last race, after all. Maybe the 50 state plan wasn't possible. Well, I'd just keep on going now. Up to this point the most I had ever run without stopping was just a little better than 23 miles. I walked up the little hill. I just couldn't get the darn legs to work. So I walked all the way until mile 25. If I could run a nine–minute mile, I still had a chance to break four hours. That would be a tough time to make. That last mile took me almost 13 minutes. It was depressing. Then I crossed the finish line and saw Jeanne and the kids cheering for me. I was euphoric. Yes, I would try for the 50 States Club.

While Jeanne stretched me at the end, I told her about my new plan.

"You want to do what?" she asked. "Well, as long as *you're* doing the running, and not me!"

This was the first run in which I saw the kids' faces at the finish, and I knew that with this new plan, I wanted to see them at all the runs. I proudly accepted my T–shirt and medal as my mind jumped ahead to the next run. I'd have to pick a state with a marathon soon. All that lay ahead with this 50 & D.C. plan was beyond comprehension at this point.

Time: 4:03:23

5

Lost
February 14, 1999

ARIZONA   ✈ 1,907 miles

So, once I was home, the idea of joining the 50 States Club took hold
with strength. Since I had to run seven more to join the group, I went
to the computer and found a Web site called "Runners' World." I figured there would be a page or two of races to choose from. I punched
"print," and twenty pages of races came pouring out of my printer, in
places I hadn't even heard of. I just had to start with one, for now.
Arizona won because it was coming up soon, and it was on a weekend when I didn't have reserve duty.

Part of the problem with my new plan was finding time to actually *go* to these events. Time for training was almost nonexistent. To
participate in the marathons, which were almost always on weekends,
I had to trade days with one of three colleagues. I was already trading
days to go to the reserves. This meant some heavy bargaining. I

offered to work two Sundays if someone would work one Saturday for me. With all the extra hours, I did experience some tough times staying alert. One of my more delusional moments took place at work about 2a.m., when everything had been done except the final inspection. Our warehouse had a rather large basement, where we stored much of our cargo. I took the large freight elevator down to it and did a quick walk around. Everything was fine. I went back onto the elevator and went up to the main warehouse floor, where we staged our cargo for morning flights. When the elevator reached the main floor and the door raised open, I stood there for a couple of seconds and peered into the warehouse. It was dark. The only light was coming from an exit sign over a door around the corner. So, basically, I could only distinguish the shapes of forklifts, bag carts and cargo. It just so happened that one item of cargo was an air tray with human remains in it. Yes, we do ship deceased bodies. While standing in the elevator and looking out to the freight, I heard what I thought was a scratching sound. The sound was coming directly from the air tray. I thought to myself, "What the hell?" I listened again, and I heard "scratch, scratch." So I walked out of the elevator toward the air tray. It was in a specially made lift that raised the air tray about six inches from the floor. I was about three feet away from it when I got down on my knees to look under it to see if there was a mouse or something under it. Again, I heard, "scratch, scratch."

This time I was sure the sound was coming from right inside that air tray. I was also sure that I needed to open it up because there was either an animal or a person alive inside. I also knew that I needed a witness before I could open it. It just so happened, that at the far end of our long building, the Chicago Police had an office. So, after about the tenth "scratch, scratch," I hurried out the door and ran down to the police department. I told the dispatcher that there was a spooky situation happening in my warehouse. I explained what I had heard. He told me to go back and wait for a unit to come over. Five minutes later two officers came over. As we were walking toward the air tray, I explained what I had heard. They both shined their flashlights at the air tray when the "scratch, scratch" noise came again.

I excitedly said, "See? That's what I've been hearing."

About then, one of the officers shined his flashlight on a box of cargo that was placed right next to the air tray. It had a bunch of little holes in it, and the label on the outside read, "LIVE TUR-TLES." I think I could have fit in that little box myself then. The officer said, "Don't worry; we won't tell anyone."

Well, the next day I woke up to find the local talk shows were having a field day with it. It even made the national news. Some of my coworkers saw it and described it as a 15–second piece with a picture of an airplane and turtles. Fortunately, the media didn't get my name or number. I would have hated to have been the butt of all the jokes on morning talk shows. I guess this could be considered my subtle way of giving some free publicity to the company I am so proud to work for.

Beyond work hours, the second obstacle was finding the funds. I calculated that the marathons were costing between seven hundred and a thousand dollars each for all expenses. The solution: even more hours of work. The extra hours to earn money for the marathons made them more special, and the time off traveling with my family, something precious. Jeanne and the kids still saw the races as long times of waiting at finish lines, but I planned to change that with the next few runs. I figured with the pace I was setting, we'd have four years of trips. It was all very exciting studying the lists, seeing trips in my head.

With the money and time off ready, we headed for Phoenix and the Desert Classic Marathon. It was a special time because it was our eleventh wedding anniversary. I wanted to make it nice for Jeanne. I knew what she wanted. She had hinted enough. She had lost the diamond out of her wedding ring at work, something that upset her terribly, but I didn't have the money to buy the kind of ring I wanted her to have. Without complaining, she works, takes care of us, attends school meetings about the children, tutors the kids, and plans the logistics of our marathon trips. Well, we'd have this trip together, and I had bought us a new camera. This time we'd bring home a scrapbook full of photos.

The album was not to happen. No sooner were we on the plane than I asked Jeanne for the camera for a shot of the city. She looked below her seat. "It's not here."

"It *has* to be," I logically announced, but, of course, it wasn't, despite what "had to be." It had gone on a trip of its own, perhaps taking photos of someone else's fabulous trip.

During my insistence that the camera must be there, I heard Erin's chorus in the background, "Are we there yet? …This trip is taking too long …Is this plane ride over?"

Eventually, the answer was yes. From the frigid February winds of Chicago, we had been transported to the welcoming sunshine of Phoenix. We went immediately to report our missing camera, but it was not coming back. Well, we'd have memories. The next stop was the auto rental desk, where we learned that our reserved car was not available and were instead offered a mini–truck with side facing seats in the back. Austin and Erin thought this was real cool, which was cause for them to chatter and giggle whenever we were driving around.

This time, we had a leisurely evening walking around Phoenix. We stopped for dinner in an Italian restaurant and finally Erin and Austin were enjoying themselves. I smiled at Jeanne, glad it was with her that I had spent these last eleven years and looking forward to whatever lay ahead.

The Run

We drove to the starting area early the following morning. It was still dark and very chilly. The temperature was 36 degrees. I couldn't wait to get started so I could warm up. It was downright cold. That's the story of deserts, hot at noon, freezing at dawn.

Finally, the gun went off, and I was on my way. I loved this flat, wide dirt path course. It was really neat absorbing the scenery. The giant cactus plants reminded me of the Road Runner show. I felt euphoric watching the sun rise with the cactus standing tall as silhouettes.

As nice as the scenery was, I was still running, not taking a Sunday stroll. I was a little out of shape for a marathon. I hadn't trained very much, since we had just gone through a blizzard in Chicago on January 1st and the running paths had been all snow. So my legs were getting heavy early on. This was at about the 10–mile mark. It was also warming up rather quickly. At about 17 miles I was hurting. I was thirsty, too. The water stops seemed to be a long way apart. I hung in there as best I could. At mile 20 I was still under three hours. I was on a sub four–hour pace. But at this point I was hurting badly. At mile 21, I realized that I was no longer sweating— a bad sign. My mouth was parched. I was dehydrating, and the day's temperature was rising. As much as I didn't want to, I knew I had to slow to a walk then. What a bummer, watching that sub–four–hour time diminish. I just couldn't do anything about it. When I finally finished the run a little after 10a.m., the temperature had risen to 80 degrees. It still felt good to cross the finish line, even though my time sucked. It was such a nice run that I figured I'd do it again someday when I was in better shape.

Time: 4:10:53

Our flight back to Chicago wasn't until 6p.m., so we hopped in our little rental truck and went for a ride. Oh, what fun it was. I loved it. The kids loved it. Jeanne hated it. We found some unpaved back roads and drove for miles. We passed a federal prison. There were signs everywhere warning drivers not to stop or pick up any hitchhikers. We found ourselves in the middle of nowhere, with no place to stop anyway.

Eventually we did find a place to stop, and despite the signs, we pulled over and got out to explore. In the sand, there were cacti of all types, some with flowers blooming, others with cactus pears on top. There were short, fat barrel cacti and the tall saguaros with arms reaching for the sky. There was food and water if someone were stranded out here. Of course we weren't stranded—at least not yet.

We jumped back in the truck and were off again, driving on a road that seemed to have no end.

Jeanne became concerned. "Shouldn't we go back now? We might miss our flight." She had asked her boss for Monday off at work, but had been told it was not possible. We had to return this night, and we would.

"No, it's not necessary to turn back," I assured her. "We'll cross a state highway soon, and it will take us back another way." However, the farther East we went, the more mountainous the road became. I didn't see a state highway. I half expected to see a "Welcome to New Mexico" sign. Finally, I had no choice. I had to turn around and head back from where we came.

Fortunately, we made it to the airport with time to spare. In the airport I bought Jeanne an anniversary gift, a small cactus plant. Later, we put it on the window sill at home, a reminder of that trip and the long drive; although I'm sure none was needed. On the flight back, the kids slept most of the way. When we were in Chicago, I asked Erin if the flight was long or short.

She smiled saying; "It was very short." I wondered why.

The next day at home, I checked out the "Map It" Web site. I pulled up the area where we had driven. It turned out that if we had driven another five miles, we would have reached the paved state highway I had expected to cross. I didn't have to tell Jeanne, "See I told you so." I just printed the map and handed it to her. She grinned, but said nothing. Of course she couldn't say anything. She likes to tell people that, in our relationship, she is always right. But—ha!—she wasn't right this time.

6

Getting It Right
March 20, 1999

VIRGINIA   ✈ **931 miles**

Our next marathon, the Shamrock Sports Fest in Virginia Beach, was cooler and more fun. It was one of our most successful and enjoyable vacations yet. I had a clear vision of what I wanted to gain from each place we were going to visit from now on. Each of us was going to learn something from everywhere we went. That was the plan, at least. I still had to see how it would work in reality.

Before the trip I had talked to Austin and Erin about the fun it would be to visit each state. However, at this stage in their lives, they couldn't really grasp all I was telling them. So far, Texas and Arizona had been mostly waiting—waiting in airports, waiting at finish lines—their least favorite activity. Jeanne absorbed the brunt of their frustrations, but she kept quiet and tolerated the inconveniences. I was determined things would be better for all of us in Virginia.

Also in the background were the worries about Austin in school. We still had not been given a diagnosis for why he had so much trouble learning, even though there had been numerous meetings with teachers, psychologists and social workers. Everyone had worries and opinions, but no one had a *why*. There had to be a reason that Austin couldn't learn as easily as other children and why his social skills were not the same. Erin had some of those same problems on a lesser scale. I decided that if they were not learning well in the usual way of reading books, maybe they could learn better with actual experiences. So, with that in mind, we started out for Virginia Beach, for both the marathon and the family trip.

To start with, this trip would not be so rushed. For the first time in over two years, Jeanne and I took a week of vacation at the same time. Also, the kids were on spring break. We flew to Norfolk and rented a car. We drove to Virginia Beach and had supper near the beach. Then we rented a nice, though economical, hotel early, so everyone would be well rested. The beach itself was beautiful; a refreshing change from Chicago.

The Run

It was cold waiting for this run to start. Once the gun went off and I started moving, I warmed right up. My first mile was just better than seven minutes. My goal was to run as many miles as possible at eight minutes each. At the 8–mile mark I was just under one hour. I was very pleased with my pace and time. This was the first run for which I used Power Gel, a gooey substance with glucose and other stuff that helped replace what I lost on the race. I had four of them from beginning to end. I just wondered at what point my legs would start getting too tight to keep the pace. This time they never got tight. I was able to keep the same pace the entire distance. It helped that the course was flat the whole way, and the temperature, a perfect 55 degrees. I was elated when I crossed the finish line under three–and–a–half hours. This was the first time I ran a marathon from beginning to end without stopping for any reason.

They were waiting for me at the finish line, and Austin and Erin had their thumbs up to touch mine, our symbol of solidarity otherwise known as a "smart." I felt great at having run at under four hours again. If I could get down to 3 hours, 10 minutes, I could qualify for Boston.
Time: 3:25:23

For now, that great feeling carried over to the rest of the vacation. As soon as the run was over, we hopped into the rental car and drove the 220 miles to Charlottesville, where we visited Monticello, home of Thomas Jefferson. I consider him one of my favorite past presidents and had just finished reading his biography. I told the kids that this was a famous home that they could see on the back of a nickel. It was so special to stand on his lawn and feel myself go back in time, imaging Jefferson there. I could have stayed much longer, but we had a dinner date with one of Jeanne's former coworkers, so I promised myself a trip back someday.

The next day was another trip back in time, in Colonial Williamsburg. There, we walked over the bridge and into the 1700s. Our guides were all dressed for the times: women in white bonnets and flowing dresses; the men in tunics and three–cornered hats. They spoke to us of events and customs of the 1700s as if we had really crossed over in a time machine. We saw candles being made, and I explained to the kids there was no electricity in those days. People made everything, including their own soap. We all tried rock candy, with the flavor taking us back in time. Nothing they could learn in school could teach them half what this visit did. Finally, we were reaping the side benefits of the marathon chase.

The following day we turned in our car and flew to Newark and on to Syracuse, New York. Syracuse was a new kind of destination. This was a trip to my own past. I wanted to see my Grandpa Keesler and also visit the farm I had lived on as a boy.

I had only seen my father's father twice before. The first time had been when Jeanne and I were visiting my mother's father, and I decided it was time to look up Dad's side of the family. I'll never forget the day, calling my Grandma Keesler, making the arrangements and actually meeting both of them for the first time. It was one of the most precious moments of my life. Although my own father had already passed away, I felt I honored him by meeting *his* parents. The second time I visited my grandfather was at my grandmother's funeral. I'm glad I had at least one occasion with her while she was alive. There are times I feel cheated, but I try not to be bitter as I continually struggle to make sense of why things happened the way they did.

Now I was here for the third time, with not only Jeanne, but Erin and Austin.

As a parent, I thought it was so important for me to make sure they had a chance to meet their great grandfather. This time, Grandpa Keesler was living in a rest home, finishing out his days in a way we all hope to avoid. Here he was, sharing a room with three other men, with only a curtain for privacy. The good part was that he was alert and knew who we were.

I took his hand and held it. "Hello, Grandpa. I'm Marlin. Remember?" He did. Having only seen me twice before, he remembered me as his son's son. His body was weak, but his mind was still sharp.

It meant so much to be there talking with him. However, to some children, a visit to the infirm elderly often involves fear and uneasiness, with no concept that someday they will also be older. It's like visiting a foreign country. Erin was one of those queasy children, and she didn't see a man who once ran across fields; she just saw old forms in bed and wanted out. "Let's go. It stinks in here." I excused us soon afterward, wishing she had kept quiet.

However, the next day, Grandpa put us at ease with his comment, "You've got to watch out with kids. Sometimes they'll put you on the spot." I was proud to be related to such a man. We wheeled in a TV and watched a show together, and then he posed for photos with the kids. Erin was especially nice to him. I was glad we had come.

I told him about the marathon I had just run in Virginia. "How long of a run is that?" he wanted to know.

"Twenty-six miles."

He was impressed. Uncle Glenn, my dad's youngest brother, who was with us, said *he* couldn't run a mile.

"I can't run twenty-six feet," Grandpa added, and we all laughed. All too soon the visit was ended, and we said our goodbyes. It was all worth the trip.

Next, I had another connection with the past to share with my family: the farm. When I was little, I had milked cows there. I had passed some of my happiest moments running for the pure pleasure of it through the fields, not even knowing anything of marathons, just running. The farm was 75 acres, and I had enjoyed every inch of it.

There was a small room in the upper part of the barn where my sisters and I played house, when times were so much simpler. There was plenty of work, including feeding the pigs, who squealed to tell on me if I neglected them, and my favorite, bringing home the cows. But mostly there was fun.

There was also unspeakable tragedy. When I was nine, my mom and dad were separated. I was living with my older sister and my Dad on the farm. We always kissed him goodnight before we went to bed, but one night he was crying when we kissed him. I had never seen him cry before.

The next morning we awoke to a commotion. Mom had come over to milk the cows. Policemen were wandering around. Why? My world was about to turn upside down. I heard a bloodcurdling scream from Mom, and then a state trooper told us what I never wanted to hear, that my father had walked out to the back pasture and shot himself. Somehow, life, for him, was more than he could bear, and he had to escape.

Soon after that we moved a number of times, ending up in Kentucky. The farm was rented and later sold. However, the memories of a childhood running across fields always returns when I'm running in marathons. I have a dream that someday I'll have the funds to buy back that farm and be its caretaker. For the time being, the people who lived there showed us around, so I could let the kids see where I started out and tell them childhood stories. It was a special part of the vacation for me.

But we had more places to visit. We drove next to an old maple sugar farm, and I let the kids see the liquid come out of the trees. They tasted the deeply sweet maple candy made into leaves and flowers, learning life through taste buds. Then we crossed the border into Canada and saw Niagara Falls from that side. The massive force of cascading waters gave us an amazing sight from a revolving restaurant atop a tall building. The perfect end to a marathon vacation, as I had envisioned they could be. If only all the other 45 plus D.C. trips could be like this one.

7

Squeezed Cheek Syndrome
April 25, 1999

MICHIGAN 265 miles

This marathon turned out to be an adventure even before it began. The run started at 8 a.m. Eastern Time on Sunday. I had to work the late shift Saturday night. Jeanne and the kids slept in the car in the parking lot at my work, waiting for me. Work was very busy all night. I had a coworker pick me up some spaghetti around 8 p.m., as I had no time to go for dinner myself. When he came back, I discovered it to be a generous portion, but swimming in hamburger grease. What could I do? I was hungry, so I made myself eat it. Finally, at 2 a.m., our freighter operation (the unloading and loading of an Air France 747 cargo jumbo jet) was complete, and I was ready to go. I figured it would take four hours to drive to the marathon start. If so, I would have an hour to spare once we arrived. We were leaving from the Central Time Zone, which made it already 3 a.m. Michigan time.

The timing would have been perfect were it not for the unexpected added challenge of a heavy fog, so I had to drive even slower than I'd planned. When I reached the final exit on I–94, I had only twenty miles to go, but it would take every minute of the last hour. I followed the map and worked my way through some back roads. About this time, Jeanne woke up and helped by giving directions. However, as I drove, I sensed that something was not right. To make a long story short, I was on the *opposite side* of the lake from where the marathon would be run. This was not going to work. Now time was really running short. I had twenty minutes to get around to the other side. It took *nineteen*. I pulled into the parking lot, quickly exchanged my work pants for running shorts, changed my socks, put the dirty ones in my pockets, stretched for 20 seconds and ran to the start line. Bang! The gun went off, and I was on my way.

The Run

Boy was I in for a run that I would not soon forget. I had just come off of my best one ever. I was looking forward to matching or bettering that time. This was my first *trail* run, and I had no idea what a trail run was like. I would soon find out. It went up and down hills and through scenic woods. The up hills were very steep. When I got to the top and started down the other side, I had to brake myself in order to keep from tripping on a tree root or rock. Avoiding the obstacles was the real challenge of this course. I ran with another runner for a little while. He told me he had done this run before. He said that the Running Fit Trail Marathon was not the one for setting a PR (personal record). He said it usually took him three months to heal from the beating the run gave him. To make matters worse, I was not in any shape for a run, even if the course were on a stadium track, thanks to the greasiest spaghetti known to man. Add the fact I'd driven five hours on no sleep and was more prepared for a nap than a marathon; but here I was, so I willed my feet to move forward. They were listening, somehow, but my stomach was protesting. I hadn't gone even a mile yet when I heard a voice. It called to me, "Come over here." So I detoured to my right and went deep into the woods. I went far enough to lose sight of the trail. Sure enough, there she was. Mother Nature was calling me, and I was happy to oblige. Thank God I had kept my socks with me that I had changed out of

earlier. Okay. Now I was good to go and on my way again. That little diversion cost me 10 minutes, but what can you do?

The trail was something else. It went up and down and down
and up. The bad part was that I couldn't pick up speed downhill,
and the up hills were very steep. Also, I had to avoid tripping on
roots and rocks in the way. It made me feel a little better to know
others had struggled on the course, too. Even though I couldn't
pick up speed, I had a comfortable pace. I still thought about those
ten minutes I had lost, when every second counted. Then it happened again. I heard that faint voice. "Come here." I ignored it. At
mile 9 it grew louder. About a half mile later, I knew for sure it was
her. I quickly ran off the trail and up the hill to my right. I was
passing an area that was mostly open field with only a couple of
trees. Oh, well. A short distance away, up the hill, I leaned my back
on the only tree around and worked my way into a sitting position.
(Aren't the details great?) I dropped my shorts and took care of
business. Another runner passed by on the trail below and saw me.
He said, "That looks interesting." Well, when Mother Nature calls,
it wouldn't be polite not to answer. I had lost five more minutes,
but I was back as soon as possible following the ups and downs of
the course. It looped around the lake two times. Therefore, the
halfway point was also the start and finish. As I neared the halfway
point, guess who I heard calling my name? No, it wasn't Jeanne
and the kids cheering me on. Yup, it was her again. The problem
was she started calling me quite a ways before the half. I was out of
socks, and I really wanted to make it to the half, so I could have
the luxury of a porta–potty. I wondered how many people had
actually run a mile with a case of "squeezed cheek syndrome." I
could now say I had. I made it just in time. I saw Jeanne at the half
and called out, "I'll be right back." The depressing part is I didn't
come right back. I spent 15 minutes in that aromatic box. One
thing was for sure—I came out empty.

At that point, I was 2 hours and 30 minutes into the run. I was
very disappointed. There was no way I would even break four hours.
I contemplated quitting. I told Jeanne as I went by that I had two
more hours to go to finish. Somehow, I hit the trail and went around
again. During the last six or seven miles, my legs started to feel
fatigued. On three occasions I actually tripped and fell. This gave me

some minor scrapes and bruises. Finally, when I didn't think I could move another muscle, I was at the finish line.

Time: 4:33:48

There was no time for seeing any sights in Michigan or even resting. We got back into the car and drove four hours back to Chicago. This was my worst run up until then. I knew it had to have been very boring for Jeanne and the kids. We would have to make another trip back to Michigan just to visit and see the state. This counted as a marathon, but it did not count as having come to Michigan.

* * * *

Three years later we *did* go back to Michigan, but just as tourists. This little excursion was definitely an oddity for us since it did not include a run. We drove the "Circle Lake Michigan" route, driving the Wisconsin side first, then the upper peninsula of Michigan. The best part was going over on a boat, like back in time, to Mackinac Island. On this tiny bit of land, travel is only by horse and buggy, tandem bikes or on foot. Erin and Jeanne pedaled one bike and Austin and I another. After so many miles, we had rushed by the world in cars and airplanes; it was inspiring to actually see the pine trees and daffodils we slowly passed. We stopped in a hotel lobby for the island's specialty: big squares of creamy chocolate fudge. While enjoying our treats in the lounge, we observed a couple of bats hanging on the ceiling. One of the hotel staff informed us that the bats were regular guests who liked "hanging out" at the hotel. After our full day on the island we crossed back over to Mackinaw City on the lower peninsula and found a campground where we pitched our tent and roasted hot dogs and marshmallows over a camp fire. Now the state could be claimed as one of our own.

8

Working Through The Numbers
May 8, 1999

WISCONSIN 49 miles

Believe it or not, after that exhausting disaster of Michigan, I was in another state, ready to run again, just two weeks later. For this one, in Lake Geneva, Wisconsin, I also had to work the night before instead of sleeping. Not a good beginning. And not a good ending, either, as I had to return to work right after the run. I had a second of doubt, but I knew that if I ever were to finish the 50 states, I had to get through the numbers, so I made plans, and we went.

Wisconsin was already familiar territory. I had my Air Force Reserve duty in Milwaukee. Fortunately, I had been allowed to bring my family, and they always enjoyed the hotel swimming pools. For my part, I felt honored to be part of the reserves, though the logistics of my complicated life made it difficult to contribute during training, especially when I worked nights, and reserve duty was during the day time.

Later, when I had to consider the possibility of being deployed overseas, I had to think seriously of the total picture. Austin's problems studying causes him to take over two hours to do the same homework that other children can complete in 20 minutes. Had I been called up, Jeanne would have been left with her job, plus *all* the tutoring of Austin as well as Erin. The total responsibility alone of both of our special needs children plus working would be very difficult for anyone, so I had no choice but to eventually resign from the reserves. But the time we *did* go to Wisconsin for reserves was a family treat.

Lake Geneva is a very nice place to visit; a clean, picturesque town with historic shops to visit. And it has a lake, as the name implies. The marathon was going to go around the lake with a couple of turnouts to complete the full distance.

The Run

My training for this run was less than for the last, plus I was tired, but the run must go on. It helped that it was out in the country. I liked running past dairy farms, where the cows could stare out at me as I stared at them. They took me back to the time when I milked ours on the New York farm and ran over those fields. My legs forgot to be tired, as I was an inexhaustible boy again. I'll never forget making a turn and facing a hill that seemed to go on forever. Then I realized, back here in this marathon in Wisconsin, I had made it up the hill without stopping or walking at all.

This event consisted of other runs. There was the marathon walk, in which the participants had a three–hour head start. There was also a marathon relay, and a half–marathon. There was even a Euro marathon, which is basically a 22–mile trail run that converged several times with my marathon course. The result was that I found myself being passed many times throughout the entire trip. These people were running past me rather swiftly. When a couple of other runners buzz by you, it's okay. When a bunch of runners buzz by you throughout the entire run, then there is a tendency to feel just a little slow. Fortunately, most of those who passed me were either relay runners or half–marathoners.

At about the 13–mile mark, five runners zipped right around me and down the hill. It turned out they were finishing the half–marathon.

At that point, there were signs that directed runners to the half–marathon finish or to continue the full marathon. It was tempting to just cross the finish of the shorter marathon. What was neat was that the five half–marathon runners in front of me were greeted by welcome cheers.

But I turned and took my path, and one of the event aids yelled, "There goes another one!" Everyone started cheering loudly and applauding. That felt really good, and I continued the full course with renewed enthusiasm. There was no one to follow now. I was on my own for at least two miles, until one of those relay runners whizzed by me again.

As I approached the finish line, my legs became tighter and sore. However, it was a pleasant place to run, a dirt path with a lake on the right. At the end, I actually passed several other runners and ran right across the line. This was only the second marathon I had completed without stopping for any reason. There was an especially nice sweat-shirt awaiting me. I was under four hours, tired, but very satisfied.

The most important part of the finish was hearing the screams of, "Good Job, Marlin!" and "Way to go, Dad!" The smiles and thumbs–up from Jeanne and the kids were special. The cheers along the way from aids and spectators were great, but the cheers from my family, yelled with love, were much better.

Time: 3:45:54

9

Cabin On The River
May 30, 1999

MINNESOTA 319 miles

Just three weeks after I'd run one in Wisconsin, I was going to another marathon. Squeezing in the 10 to join the 50 States Club was becoming a rush, but I was still determined. This one, the Med–City Marathon, was on bike paths through a local park in Rochester, Minnesota.

Before the race, however, we had a chance to enjoy the mini vacation in a different way from hotels. A friend at work, Weldon, had lent us his cabin set on a bluff in Wisconsin, about two hours from Rochester. The cabin overlooked the Mississippi River with a breathtaking view. Eagles flew above us, a sign of good luck. We had two days to relax. At night, we took jars and ran around catching fireflies. They were everywhere, even landing lightly on our hands. With flashlights, we walked on gravel paths greeted by deer and wild turkeys.

When the day came to run, I added to the excitement of the drive with my strong determination. This is a good trait when running a marathon, but it's not the best when deciding that you don't want to buy gas until you absolutely have to. As I drove us down from the cabin to Rochester in our Saturn station wagon, I decided to get as close as possible before stopping for gas. We crossed the river and drove up the Iowa side to Minnesota, catching I–90 West within a few miles. Gas stations were everywhere on the interstate. I could pick and choose. I looked at the tank: one fourth full. No problem. I could drive about 30 more miles. I did. Then there was a problem. We were in the middle of a Minnesota plain, and there were no gas stations at all, in any direction. There were exits to visit someone's farm, but not to buy gas. Apparently, you were supposed to fill up before coming to this isolated area. Finally, there was a sign for a small town at the next exit, six miles away. I took it. There, in the middle of a few houses that passed for a town, was a mom and pop shop with a gas pump, and a large, hand–made sign: "Closed." There was no use telling myself what I *should* have done. I knew. Except for a few moans and groans, the family politely kept quiet, avoiding the obvious, "You should have…" There was nothing to do but get back on I–90 and pray a little. We moved along, as I held my breath, hoping. One more exit. Off I went and looked around. This little town had an open gas station, which I welcomed like a marathon finish line, and filled up. The tank was super–thirsty. Had the station been closed, I would have made it only about a mile. We would have been stranded somewhere in nowhere.

While our car had its marathon, the clock was ticking for the start of mine. I was supposed to arrive 30 to 45 minutes ahead of time. When we finally parked four blocks away, I had just five minutes for a nature call at a fast–food place, some stretching, and my arrival at the starting line. With the last 30 seconds, I caught my breath and readied myself mentally.

The Run

The Med–City course was nice. I was running on tree–lined, up and down, small rolling hills. The first half went well; my legs worked fine. The halfway point crossed the starting point, so I could say, "Hi," to Jeanne and the kids. The second half went in a different direction and was a little tougher. I lost most of my time in the last six miles. The temperature was perfect for running, but it was windy.

Around mile 24 I was crossing a bridge when the wind blew the hat off the man in front of me. Without hesitating a second, I turned around, chased his hat and gave it to him. That extra exertion was tough, and probably cost me a minute extra, but I thought it was the thing to do for another runner. Despite that, I finished the run under my goal for four hours.

Time: 3:51:42

Now that the run was completed, I relaxed. I wanted the family to have a taste of Minnesota beyond searching for gas and watching me run. I took them to the Mall of America, where a giant Snoopy reigns over the seven–acre, indoor theme park, Camp Snoopy. There, they were able to run all over, ride on the merry–go–round, go down the log shoot—in general, forget school and just be kids. It was fun to watch something that crossed generations, because few can resist the lovable Snoopy.

10

An Ostrich Cheers
August 29, 1999

NEBRASKA

461 miles

With June and July to rest, I was ready for another marathon in August. The chosen state, Nebraska, has plenty of wide open spaces to run, but they put us in a great spot, running through the middle of a zoo. This was another rushed trip, with as much racing to arrive as to complete the course. However, the kids did have a hotel with a pool, which makes it a vacation for them, especially in August. They splashed each other and screamed and yelled with joy until I thought the managers would throw us out, but I guess with televisions and air conditioning, no one noticed. I was delighted to hear them so happy. I would have pulled them out if anyone had complained, though. The two are best friends, each feeling comfortable with another child with whom there is no worry about what to do or say.

We didn't see anything else in Omaha except the hotel pool, but I'm sure if I had planned better, there would have been worthwhile sights. There was an air show going on at the nearby Air Force base. Time constraints kept us from attending. What I did notice was the Mutual of Omaha building, which brought back memories of Mutual's Wild Kingdom show. I used to watch that with my sisters, when the narrator, Marlin Perkins, would leave his sidekick Jim exposed to the dangers of the wild African plains, attempting to get as close as possible to the mighty lions. It was pleasant eating popcorn next to the fireplace, always in suspense, wondering if Jim would be eaten by the lion or bitten by a snake. We all had our fair share of chores, but we were always home in front of Wild Kingdom on Sunday nights.

Now, I'd like to watch those adventures with my own kids, but when I told them about the show, it was, "The Wild *What* Show?" Some things you would like to stay the same, so two or three generations can share the same experiences. I believe marathons are one of those treasures. People were running them a generation ago, and they'll be running them a generation from now.

The Run

Omaha's run was very scenic and enjoyable, and part of it went through the zoo. I passed elephants and lions, as if running through my childhood show. As I ran, an ostrich ran along its side of the fence as if it were cheering me on. There were runners in front of me and behind me, but for some reason that ostrich chose to run alongside me. This was a very cool experience. But it was not all a fun trip through the zoo. After that, the course went across the Missouri River and into Iowa. (This should have given me two states in one, as at least half the race was in that state.) In Iowa it was mostly flat, although I had to go up and down a couple of challenging hills back on the Nebraska side. However, there was enough flat to give me a good finish time. I crossed the line, pressed thumbs with my private cheering squad and stretched out.

Time: 3:51:36

Then it was back in the car for the ride in reverse. This time there was not only the feeling of unbelievable fatigue, but I felt a shooting pain down my right leg as I drove. I knew something was definitely wrong. There was. It turned out to be a protruding disc in my lower back. Were my marathon days over before I had even made the 10 runs for the Club?

11

Fond Memories
September 18, 1999

OHIO

370 miles

The pain was still there when the drive was over, and long after. I went to a chiropractor, who put me on physical therapy, but told me, "No more marathons." This was not what I wanted to hear, especially since the run next month was special. It was the Air Force Marathon in Ohio, where I first met Jeanne.

No, I couldn't quit now. Somehow I'd run that one, and *then* I'd talk to more doctors. For now, Jeanne and I were gong to relive old memories and make some new ones. I could remember like yesterday coming to Ohio in '84, a young man who had just joined the Air Force. Earlier that year I had ridden my motorcycle across the United States to go live with my sister in California. Immediately, I found work vacuuming carpets and pushing shopping carts in a department store parking lot. I soon realized that I couldn't make ends meet doing that, so I walked right into an Air Force recruiting station and soon found myself in San Antonio, Texas for basic training. I had a place to sleep, food to eat three times a day, and I was getting paid for it. This worked. What I didn't have was a girlfriend, someone to share life with.

For this, I needed to be in Ohio, where my lifetime love was waiting, unknown to me. The Air Force helped by stationing me at Wright–Patterson Air Force Base in Fairborn, Ohio. While there, I was headed to watch a Led Zeppelin concert on a friend's TV when my car wouldn't start. I jump started it and was driving around to charge the battery up, when I picked up another friend. We never made it to hear the concert. Instead, we went to visit a friend of his, Terri. There, I was introduced to Terri's sister, Jeanne. I saw warmth in her eyes from the beginning, as her melodic voice asked, "Do you know what your name means?" Of course I did, but I pretended I didn't. I needed something to talk about as she led me to a book full of names and their meanings. I'm an introvert by nature, but Jeanne didn't need me to start the conversation. She was plain fun. We laughed and talked until midnight, when my friend said we had to go. Before I left, however, Jeanne and I had set up a time to see a movie the next night.

When my friend and I were in the car, I turned on the radio and the Beatles were singing, "Birthday." At the stroke of midnight, I turned 20. The best years of my life had begun.

Jeanne and I began dating, and on Valentine's Day, 1988, we were married, and Jeanne was a beautiful bride. The priest, Father Pat, who had let me live at his rectory during my junior year of high school, performed the ceremony. Jeanne and I honeymooned in Hawaii, the home of my first marathon. I never could have imagined then that someday we'd be back as residents and I would be running marathons.

Shortly after we were married, I left active duty in the Air Force and went to work for Continental Airlines at the Cincinnati Airport. We moved to Lawrenceburg, Indiana, 20 miles away, where we lived for three years. Jeanne worked full time, and I worked two full–time jobs and went to school. Even though we were away from home for so many hours, Jeanne wanted a dog because she'd always had one as a child. I resisted; she insisted. Then, one afternoon, when she came home she almost tripped over her surprise, a tiny puppy, which she named Fuzzhead. The pup was treated almost like a child, and was soon joined by our son, Austin, who arrived on Thanksgiving Day, 1989. Despite how tough things were, we were happy just being life partners.

In September 1999 we were again in Ohio, this time with both our children, and a love made even stronger by all we'd been through together. This was, again, a marathon with little sleep. The drive was painful. Both my leg and hip hurt as I drove, but I was determined to make this run, so I pushed on. We arrived at Jeanne's parents' house tired, but to a family welcome. It was after midnight, so I went straight to bed, where my tired muscles relaxed the minute I touched the soft mattress. I caught a couple hours of sleep before being ready to stand on the starting line at 5a.m.

During the pre–dawn stretching, I met a lady who was chauffeuring her 14–year–old son, Brenton Floyd, to marathons. He wanted to break the record of the youngest person to complete all 50 states. He did break that record and set new ones. I had my own record, just being able to run at all with this pain.

The Run

The run was nice. I really enjoyed running through all the places I had traveled on my daily Air Force routine. At the beginning, we were at the top of a steep hill. I ran down it fairly easily, and then the course was flat. The worst problem was getting back up that hill at the end. There were plenty of water stations and porta–potties strategically placed. I had to stop for one at the 17 mile marker. I hate when that happens, but when Nature calls, she wants an answer. It ruins my time. After that, I had a hard time getting going again. My pace diminished. My legs were so sore that I had to walk most of the hill at mile 24. I was so close to a sub four–hour finish, but my legs just wouldn't work. They hurt awfully. The time of four hours was sneaking up on me. As I went down the other side of that hill, I had to finally admit to myself that I wasn't going to break four hours. I was actually walking beside a lady who had a similar goal. She wished me luck and started running again. I watched her get farther and farther away, while my feet were still walking slowly one in front of the other.

Now there were many runners passing me. Somewhere around mile 25, I reached down deep inside me and found the strength to run again. Oh, boy, did it hurt. I realized I still had a chance to break four hours. As I neared the finish line I passed the lady who had walked with me earlier. What a thrill it was to cross that finish line and be able to rest. I had done it in just under four hours. I had a minute to spare. Now I had 10 states. It gave me a huge psychological boost to know I was now eligible. I *can* do this. I really can. I didn't join right away, but it made me feel good to know that I could. Now I had to get rid of some pain, so I could look for a new state.

Time: 3:58:11

12

GEORGIA ✈ 776 miles

Despite wanting to head for number 11, my body and life demand-
ed I take a break. More than a year passed before I ran again. For one,
there was no money for running. There was barely enough money for
living. We were broke, and I had to work as much as possible to keep
us afloat. Time off for the joy of running was a luxury I couldn't think
about for a while. Secondly, I still had my injuries. I realized my back
problem was from an injury suffered while working on a cargo
freighter. It didn't seem too bad at the time, but it became continually worse. The back pain would shoot down my right leg, but strangely I only felt it when driving, not when running. I first noticed it driving home from the Omaha marathon in August of '99. After the Air
Force marathon, I had to give up training altogether. I had an MRI
which showed a protruding disc in my lower L–5 spine area. I didn't

need a test to know something was not right, but it helped the doctors see that there really was a cause for pain. I continued therapy and tried to improve the way I moved my body at work to exert the least amount of stress on my back. This seemed to help. By spring of 2000, I no longer had the shooting leg pains. But I wasn't to stay pain–free for long. In February, while pushing a freighter pallet that wouldn't budge, I felt my right knee pop. After that, I mostly pushed with my left leg, but then that knee popped. Doctors are not my cup of tea, so, again, I didn't rush to see one. Maybe I'd get better exercising the knees. All spring and summer I tried to train again. The knees were having none of it. They were on strike, giving me the message that I had to see a doctor, like it or not.

Thirdly, we still had not received any good advice on dealing with Austin's learning problems. No one had yet given us the name "Asperger's Syndrome." When we were finally given the name, we also learned that it is a form of high functioning autism. But at this time, we didn't even have a name. We just knew something wasn't right. He wasn't learning as he should, and he was not very social with other children. As he complained, "I don't understand," or, "I can't do it," I just became more frustrated. Was I doing something wrong? Why couldn't I get through to him? I'd get angry, which helped even less. I'd have trouble staying awake while helping him with his homework because of all the hours I was working. It would have been difficult enough if I were tutoring a child I didn't know in an after–school program, but this was my own son, who looked like me, who looked up to me. I should be able to communicate, to help him.

Whatever I had learned in school, it had not prepared me to pass on that knowledge to someone who needed special help. Then, if I went running on an afternoon, I felt guilty that I wasn't there with him, although my help was not getting the work done. The situation played on my conscience. We continued to go to round table meetings with psychologists, teachers, social workers—people who should have known, I thought, what to do. It wasn't something he was going to "grow out of." All we could do was give him love. The marathons were a way for all of us to interact without any pressures of school or homework. I didn't have to be forcing him to learn anything. It just came naturally when we traveled.

Erin, too, we later concluded, has Asperger's. In addition, she has Turner Syndrome, where a missing chromosome in women causes stunted growth and other physical abnormalities. As with Austin, we knew she learns better verbally—listening, talking—so our trips were good for them both.

In addition, I learned later that Austin's lack of social interaction with his peers was part of Asperger's, but I didn't know it then. I saw he reacted better with his little sister and with us. The literature I would later read said the same thing. The children feel less pressure with people younger and older than they are. So for both these reasons, the informal learning and the family social interaction and trips together for the marathons were the ticket.

I would *have* to squeeze one into the year 2000. With sore knees and all, I started training again, setting my sights on a run I read of for November in Atlanta. I didn't know that another adversity was on its way.

Everything tried to stop us, but my mind was made up. The sewer backed up in the house, and I had to pull out all the carpet from the basement. The carpet was old and smelly, and I did the work with no protective filter mask. Result: I breathed the molds and particles in the air. Soon, I had a mild cough, but I didn't want to miss the marathon. I hoped it would go away.

On the 22nd of November, we flew to Atlanta. After visiting Jeanne's long distance coworker friend, we went to Stone Mountain. We learned of Stone Mountain from a library book about Georgia that Austin brought home from school. He was proud of the contribution he made to our travel plans. That's where Confederate soldiers are carved in the side of a mountain. As I watched Erin and Austin laughing beside us on the tram to the top, I knew I'd made the right decision. Like their trip back in time in Virginia, this was certainly more memorable than a history chapter in a book. We also made a visit to the CNN building and watched a little news.

It was great to be back traveling with them, but there was one problem I could no longer ignore: my cough was becoming worse. By night time it was so severe I couldn't sleep at all because of the violent spasms of coughing. It was like what I had heard of whooping cough, but I'd had my shots as a baby. Something was seriously wrong, but did I go to a doctor? You must know me by now. I took our rental car to the starting area for the marathon instead.

The early morning was chilly, so I sat in the car a while with the heater on, still coughing. About a half–hour before the run, I got out, stretched, and did some short sprints. By this time, I realized I was also having trouble breathing. I gave up on stretching and went back to the car. I contemplated not running at all, but this was my last chance to run in 2000. I could start it and see how far I'd go. Yes, I *would* go on.

The Run

The starting gun went off, and I was on my way. Instantly, I realized I was having a difficult time breathing again. I just couldn't get a deep breath in. On some of my training runs, I had been out of breath in the first few miles until I settled down. I hoped I would reach that point this time. I remember telling another runner that I now understand the old commercial that said something like, "When you can't breathe, nothing else matters." I just could not breathe well enough. This caused me to run a steady, but soft pace.

I decided that at the 5–mile mark, I would quit if I still couldn't get my breath. I arrived there with effort, and I couldn't get air to go deep into my lungs. I assessed the situation. The rest of my body was fine. I had miracle straps on my knees, so they weren't bothering me at all. It was do or die. It would be very depressing to quit now.

I stayed focused and went on, passing the 6–mile sign, then the 7–mile one. I didn't think about time, just breathing and moving forward. Somewhere past the 20–mile mark, I started thinking of time and realized I was at a four–hour pace. My personal goal had always been to keep it under four hours since the first time I'd made it. Now, right at the end, I saw they'd put in a hill. They weren't going to stop me with that. I gave it my all for the last half mile, and I crossed the finish line with ten seconds to spare! Until then, it was the most gratifying feeling I have ever felt on a run.

This day had more to offer. It was also Thanksgiving Day and Austin's birthday. We all went to Planet Hollywood for a birthday meal and on to see Jim Carey in "How The Grinch Stole Christmas." I coughed the whole time, but other than that, I was glad to be there with my special three.

The year 2000 was a challenge, to say the least. Seven months earlier, in April, my mother tragically lost her life in an automobile accident. I had not seen her in 12 years, and she never knew either one of her grandkids. Strangely enough, her passing brought me closer to her own siblings in a way that would have a wonderful impact on our quest for 50. Her passing also gave me one final opportunity to visit my Grandpa Keesler, who passed away from pneumonia later that June. After my mother's memorial, my oldest sister, Kathleen, and I drove to New York to visit him at the rest home. This would be only the fourth time I had visited my grandfather. I was so thankful for that opportunity. The Atlanta run was dedicated to you, Gramps.

Considering all the adversities and challenges to even arrive at my only marathon during 2000, it always seems like a miracle that I made it all the way at all, even more that it was under four hours. Admittedly, I used poor judgment on my breathing problem. I should have seen a doctor sooner. Finally, when we were home, I went to a doctor and heard the news, "You have pneumonia. I'll write you a prescription, and a note for work. Marlin, this is serious." I think I was glowing when I told him I had just run a marathon with pneumonia. I don't know if he wanted to congratulate me or test my mental faculties. I was proud, although to this day I still can't believe I did it.

Time: 3:59:49

Of course Jeanne felt it necessary to update her mom on this excursion. Somewhere in that conversation I overheard her say something to the effect that, "I'm always right, mom, and you can tell him he needs to listen to me." At about that time, she handed me the phone. With a stern tone my mother-in-law said, "Marlin, what's this I hear you ran with P–na–monia? You need to take better care of yourself and listen to your wife because you know she is always right. Now let me talk to her again." I thought to myself, "Right about what?" Of course I really didn't care that they were ganging up on me. I was in bed being waited on hand and foot. I would be lying if I said I didn't enjoy it.

13

Erin's The Star
February 4, 2001

NEVADA   1,803 miles

After Atlanta, I knew I had to take care of my health if I wanted to run in more than one marathon a year. I had only run 11. Running only one a year, I'd be *seventy–two* years old running the last one. Although I'd seen runners that age in marathons, I wanted to complete my goal much sooner. The pace had to pick up.

I had signed up for the Nevada race before I even went to Atlanta. Our wedding anniversary is the most important holiday of the year to me. We always try to do something special on that day. The Las Vegas run was in February. That would work for a romantic place. Although I still didn't have the money for the kind of diamond I wanted to buy her, I'd show her a good time.

However, before I could think about Las Vegas, I had to recover from the pneumonia. I did spend a couple weeks where all I did after work was rest—no training. After that, when I felt up to running, the weather had other ideas. It dumped buckets of snow on Chicago throughout the month of December. There was nowhere to run. I tried once to run in the snow covered path of Busse Woods, but then I came down with strep throat. This was much worse than pneumonia. It knocked me flat until the day we were to leave for Las Vegas. I was going to a marathon barely recovered and with almost no training.

By not training, I had let my weight slide up. I was up to 180 pounds, the heaviest of my life. Everything was stacked against a run, but on the other side, I had my fierce determination. I *was not* not going to run.

But before I had the race, we crossed another finish line—finally finding out why Austin had such trouble in school. It was an unbelievable relief to know. He had been attending school in the regular classrooms, but it was a struggle every day. We had meetings with teachers and specialists, but no one could explain the problem. It wasn't full–fledged autism, it wasn't ADD, but it was something. Now in the fifth grade, we were in yet another meeting. This time it was different. Austin was sent to a doctor, who referred him to the psychology department at the University of Illinois. I will always be grateful to the specialists who gave us the key to helping Austin. Dr. Anita Hurtig and her intern, Erin Telford, identified the correct label. Erin took him in a room and administered test after test. At the end, she let us know, "Your son has Asperger's, a high functioning form of autism."

"He has what?" She explained some, but then she sent us to a group meeting where we bought a book on the topic. As we read, it was as if the author, Tony Atwood, had met Austin personally. Children with Asperger's have difficulty with social interactions, and among other things, have what we consider little "common sense." We went back to his school, and the next year, he was put in special education classes. He's been doing well since. Reading the book, Jeanne and I also realized that Erin has the same thing but with many different characteristics compared to Austin. She was given a teacher's aide, who helped her individually during class. Now with this matter put in its place, we could relax a little. It was time to enjoy a trip of fun, and Las Vegas was the place to do it.

Arriving at night, we drove our rented car down the strip, where the flashing colored lights of the hotels gave the impression we had landed on another planet. There were extravagant casinos pretending to be New York City or Paris, and a pyramid casino bringing Egypt to this desert. We drove by it all, but we chose a hotel off the strip and nearer to the starting line of the marathon.

Slot machines were everywhere, even in the laundromats and convenience stores. Jeanne and I took turns, one watching the kids while the other took $25–worth of quarters to feed the ever–hungry machines. Of the $50 between the two of us we won back $20, which makes one feel somewhat a winner, although we'd just lost $30 of course. But the machines were well–fed and happy.

The next morning, leaving the machines to others, we moved to a spot where the kids could join us, Hoover Dam. There, after seeing the huge Lake Mead, we put on hard hats and went down to see the enormous generators. A life–size lesson in electrical power. Our guide would occasionally question us to see if we were listening. Austin was listening. He answered one of the questions right and gloated about it the rest of the tour. Hoover Dam was a very impressive place, so I felt good knowing I had scored points with my crew.

Although making electricity for millions is magic, once back in the city, we went to a real magic show, this one by Steve Wyrick. We were amazed as he walked through turbine engines unhurt (don't try that one) and gasped as he appeared overhead, dangling from a rope. But for us, the best part of the show was when he asked for a little girl as a volunteer. He first invited the girl in front of us, but she just wiggled further down in her seat. She wanted no part of a show. Right behind her was Erin, who *was* ready and willing. She jumped up gladly when asked and ran up to the stage. We never understood how, but he actually made her levitate. It was such a treat for Jeanne and me to watch. Austin liked it at first, too, but as he watched, jealousy was beginning to sneak in. When everyone clapped for Erin and she was given a door prize of a Steve Wyrick magic kit, the jealousy was full–blown. That night, Austin pouted terribly, frustrated by what he couldn't change. He didn't want to talk. He didn't want to eat. It took most of the next day to get him normal again. We kept things low key, with room service and television, not rushing anywhere.

I was the only one who went out. I took this quiet time as a chance to visit a friend who, unfortunately, was in the federal prison north of Vegas. His wife had been Austin's kindergarten teacher, and he had been part–owner of the company I worked for in Hawaii. He is a nice guy who should not have been where he was; a disgruntled employee who screwed up got away with blaming the boss. My friend deserved a visit from a friendly face, so I hope I made a positive difference by going. For myself, I had a new appreciation for being able to run outdoors and to be with my family.

The Run

After the tours and the visit, I was now ready to run—well, as ready as I could be with almost no training. Despite being out of shape, I wanted to keep my time under four hours again. Fat chance! I might not have been ready, but the morning was—a bright, clear day with only a slight chill. So, I began. I went at a soft pace, but right away I could feel the extra weight I was carrying. My whole body felt weak. I knew this run would be a difficult one, too. As with all runs, I focused on just one mile at a time. I can't get to the next mile until I finish the one I'm on, so I went little by little, always going forward.

Once over the hill around mile nine, the ground was easier, flat or even downhill, and I had a good view of the Vegas strip. It was great just to be part of this, if my body would just cooperate. No way. Instead, my legs got tighter and tighter. Despite that, I made it to halfway in two hours. I should have been able to make less than four hours if I were feeling right, but I wasn't. I had to walk. I hate that. Time passed, and I was a long way from the finish. I thought of Jeanne and the kids waiting patiently at the line, watching other runners come in, but not seeing me. Finally, I saw them and picked up to a trot for the last few feet as I made it across to their cheers and raised thumbs. I was ready to collapse.

Time: 4:51:42

This marathon woke me up. I *had* to be able to train, and, as my mother–in–law had insisted, be healthy. "For April's run, I'll be ready to go." I said aloud. "Sure, Dad."

"Of course, Marlin."

"You can do it, Dad."

I hoped saying it aloud would give it a better chance of coming true.

14

Stretching By A Tombstone
April 28, 2001

TENNESSEE 531 miles

I was coming off my worst run ever, but at least I had time to train a little, and I had even lost 10 pounds. I would have liked to have lost more. It was a start.

For this trip, we rented a Ford Explorer and drove through my old state of Kentucky on the way to Tennessee. As I crossed the miles, I saw heading the other way the younger Marlin rushing down the same road toward California on a patched–together motorcycle. I liked my new side of the road better.

When we finally arrived in the country music capital of Nashville, we sang along with the sounds on the radio. Then I decided it was time for my favorite carb, spaghetti, which I always had eaten, even before I'd heard of marathons. So I invited the family to The Old Spaghetti Factory, a few blocks from the state capitol. It's in a row of buildings that have been there almost since the Civil War, decorated with iron trim and inviting us inside. They served many styles of the food that crosses all generational gaps. It was not the meal to lose more pounds, but I rationalized that I was about to run it off. Then we headed to a hotel near the starting line, and even closer to the finish line. (The better to reach a bed and shower sooner.)

The Run

The official marathon photographers were also there, and they gave me a ride to the start. This was a large field, with runners of all types, including Dolly Parton look–alikes. I was here, so I'd run. However, for some reason, my heart just wasn't into this run. I wanted to quit before it even started. I wanted to quit even more after it started. It just feels so good to stop, and I didn't need to run 26 miles to get that feeling. It took two minutes just to cross the start line. Within the first mile, I had to stop in the bushes. I wasn't able to settle my breathing down until I reached the 7–mile mark. Hmm. All right, maybe I'd go a little farther. My decision was helped by the bands on the sidelines playing upbeat music that spurred us on. I actually enjoyed the run while they were playing. But by mile 19, my legs were feeling sore. I had to slow down to a walk, alternated with running and back to walking again. This pace was not helped by the temperature, which had risen to 80 degrees by then, and the arrival of numerous hills. I knew I probably wouldn't break four hours this time. However, I hadn't quit. Seeing my three–person cheering squad at the finish, I sped up to a run to cross the finish line and joined them. I had made it all the way, which was enough for now. I could think about making better time on the next run. Now, I would relax.

Time: 4:09:14

The next day it was back up through Kentucky. This time, I showed the kids a couple of homes where I'd lived and bent their ears with "When I was a boy, I used to…" stories. My childhood work became legendary. I told them how I used to have to hang heavy tobacco leaves. They were glad they had missed that "fun." I recounted that the cut tobacco was spiked on five–foot long poles and passed up to workers on beams in the barn. You had to balance yourself on two beams at a time, four feet apart, a circus act. The guys on the lower tiers had to lay tobacco on their row as well as pass up to the next rows. Those on the top just had to lay it. That was for me. I climbed up to the highest tier. My hesitation stated the obvious. I was scared of heights. I grabbed a support beam with one hand and received the tobacco with the other. The boss came in and screamed, "Get him off the top!" I was only too glad to come down and work from the ground. Working extra hard on the bottom wasn't the only price I had to pay because of my fear of heights. "The man above me rained sweat down on me like a regular waterfall," I told the kids, who laughed imagining the scene, which was funny if you weren't there.

The main advantage to such tales is not that the kids learn how to hang tobacco. First, they may appreciate the lives they do have, and second, perhaps they can realize, "He's *old*," and he was a child once. Conclusion, one day I'll be *old*, like he is." Hmm. It could set them thinking. If not, it gave me a minute's pause thinking of their futures. For now, I would give them great memories.

As part of visiting my old town, I wanted to visit my stepfather's grave. The man had done his best to support my mom, always bringing home his paycheck to her hands. I thought that he should have been laid to rest in New York, near his family, but his stone was here. It had been one year since my mother had been killed in that tragic automobile accident. Although her name had been engraved next to Hal's, without a death date, her ashes were placed on top of my dad's casket in upstate New York. Even though it had been more than 12 years since I had seen or spoken to my mother, this run was in honor of her and my stepfather (Laura and Harold).

While there, my hip was aching terribly, and I was afraid my old pain would again shoot down my legs, so I asked Jeanne to stretch my legs. As I lay on the fresh green grass of Hal's grave, I felt better with the stretching. In fact, after that date, my hip has never bothered me again. (A visit from the twilight zone?)

I was then up to more travel, so I drove us to Louisville, where friends from our days in Hawaii live. Erin played with their daughter Laurel, looking for tent worms, and Austin ran around the yard with their son Zach. It was a chance to just be kids, and with individual well–known peers, not large school groups. I wanted to stay longer, but there was cargo that would be arriving in the Chicago O'Hare airport, and it would need me there. While working, my mind could start planning the next run, this time much farther away.

15

The Midnight Sun
June 23, 2001

ALASKA   3,550 miles

Alaska was a run for which I had time to train. Surely, I thought, I'd be able to make it in less than four hours. However, during the four days before the run, I drove the family around in an RV, eating and relaxing—the opposite of training—but at least I was mentally ready. It would be our best vacation to date.

After flying first class from Minneapolis, thanks to employee airline passes, I rented an RV in Anchorage. We traveled 1,100 miles in five days. It was made easier by the fact that this was summer in Alaska, the land of the midnight sun. We waited up on summer solstice to see the sun set from about 10:00 to midnight. The sky never really got dark. By about 12:40 a.m., the sun had returned, rolling back along the horizon. There were plenty of daylight hours for fun, and we used most of them.

We went camping, finding a site where there was no one else. After Chicago, wide open spaces were inspiring. We all worked to search for scarce firewood, and the reward was a large bonfire over which we roasted marshmallows and hot dogs and talked about how great the trip was already. Then we ran around in the snow in our shorts, throwing snowballs. Erin adored having the full attention of her brother, as well as her parents. No jobs, no friends of Austin's coming over for video games, just the four of us.

The second day we went to a reindeer farm, where a newborn reindeer was struggling for air in what it considered heat (about 70 degrees). Its mother stood protectively by, in case any tourist dared approach too close. After posing for photos with Rudolph and all of his reindeer friends, we headed east of Anchorage, toward a park with horses to ride.

Just the idea of riding a horse excited Erin. She kept repeating over and over, "This is the best idea, Dad, the best!" She was so excited about going horseback riding she could hardly contain herself. My head swelled with pride for making such a great choice of activity. I

learned later that many programs for children with special needs include horseback riding. It gives them a sense of being in control and a sense of height. At that time, I was just delighted that I had chosen something she was so enthusiastic about. Finally, we arrived, and she gladly let herself be lifted onto the horse. A guide had to lead her around, but still, she was sitting alone on the horse—quite a thrill. Austin was able to actually ride by himself, a real cowboy, but Erin was the happiest.

That night we went to another campground, where I saw an old abandoned school

bus that some hippies, I guessed, had once made into a mobile home of sorts. I especially liked their large bumper sticker: "I love airplane noise." People after my own heart. That's when we waited all night to see the slow sunset, the sun rolling over the horizon to hide for less than an hour.

On the third day, we had a picnic on a cliff 200 feet above a river, an awesome view for those with strong stomachs like we have. The kids seemed game for anything, so I scheduled a ride on the rapids. The water was freezing cold, but they kept demanding the guide for, "More splashes," and "Hit a bigger rapid."

We were all soaked, but it was worth it watching them giggle. After that, we made a stop at a sled dog farm, where the two were

pulled on a special track by the dogs. As chairman of our entertainment committee, I next stopped at a sports store for fishing equipment. Then we drove to look for a spot. We passed one place where fishermen were lined arm–to–arm in rows by the water, all casting lines with hooks. I didn't like the looks of "combat" fishing. We kept driving, but instead of a fishing ground, we found a wreck, caused by a tourist stopping his car in the middle of the road to photograph a moose. When the smashed cars were towed, we went instead to a nearby restaurant for already–caught fish.

That night, the three had been tourists long enough. They all fell asleep early, despite the sunlight. I still wanted to see more, so I went back to the restaurant, where weathered guys who must have started their band in the '50s were blasting out rock and roll music and people were dancing. This state was awake at all hours. I could get used to this place.

However, I had come to run, so the next day I planned a short tour of Anchorage and got a little rest myself. We still managed to see the science center and buy souvenirs, a requirement for visitors. I was now ready to run, although I had barely slept. I was energized.

The Run

When I started the run, the weather was perfect for a marathon, 58 degrees and not a cloud in the sky. The course was scenic, 26 miles straight ahead, no turning back on itself. It felt great to be out there. I had to make two porta–potty stops along the way, which cost me 10 minutes. Bummer. After mile 21 it was much harder to start again. My legs felt much tighter, so I had a tough time after that, but I kept running. I never slowed to a walk. The park we were running through was breathtaking, and a lady run up beside me yelling, "Go on. You can do it. Go for it." That felt good. Her encouragement pushed me up over the final short, steep hill, otherwise known as 'insult hill'. I even passed others as I rushed toward the finish and my awaiting family.

Time: 3:56:30

Going home, we again used our employee travel benefits, as long as we were willing to take the long way around. We went from Anchorage to Houston to Newark to Chicago, but there were no complaints. This trip was rated an A–plus. We will most definitely return someday.

16

Ticks, Heat, and an Arch
September 3, 2001

MISSOURI

416 miles

With this run I was confident of a 3:30 finish. I had trained more for this one than any other, and my weight was down to 158. Also, in preparation, I had bought us a new Ford Windstar van. No more renting cars. We put in our CDs and listened to Juice Newton, The Cranberries, The Eagles and other soft rock music, and headed down the highway.

Because it's so famous, we had to stop along the way to visit the Gateway Arch in St. Louis. This is a unique design that gives the city a landmark. Below the arch, there's the interactive Museum of Westward Expansion, where we saw letters Lewis and Clark wrote to President Jefferson about their explorations and Native American Peace Medals they received in trading. Lifelike animatronics figures, like in Disney World, told us about their lives in the past, and we

looked inside a covered wagon. Whoa! I was glad I didn't have to travel to marathons in that one. Talk about a bumpy ride. The tires were
made of wood. Although still not that crazy about heights, I put
myself to the task of riding up to the top of the arch with everyone.
Erin was kind of scared, too, so I forgot my queasy stomach while I
assured her that everything was all right. I feel good having kids I can
protect and at the same time show new places. That's what I enjoy in
these marathon trips. I wish someone had shared this kind of time
with me when I was a kid, but I can do it now. We always have today
to treasure, even if the past failed us.

     From sightseeing, which we really liked, we had to move on to
Columbia to check out my running course. I was going to run that?
It was scenic, all right, but with huge hills, six of them, with the steepest at the halfway mark. Oh, well. I'd been training. Piece of cake,
right? I could think about those hills when I was actually on them.
Now I needed a pre–run relaxation, and the kids needed to stretch
their legs. We chose a state park with a cave. The path to the cave had

a wooden walkway to guide us, but Austin and Erin decided to choose their own path to explore, and they wandered everywhere, as if they were our ancestors sent to map the place. I thought this exploration had been good for them until, on our return in the van, I heard Erin scream, "Get them off me! Get them off me!" She was kicking and stomping. I pulled over and Jeanne looked back to see what was happening. "There're spiders all over me. Get them off!" She continued to holler in fear. We looked closer, and then we saw them. Her socks and shoes were covered with thousands of tiny ticks. She was completely infested. Quickly, we pulled off her shoes and socks, and then I drove to where she could shower and then jump in a pool. It was only a five–minute drive but, for all of us, it was the longest five minutes of the trip. Later, I had to fumigate our new van. Now I was ready to do nothing more than rest until it was time to make the run. As I relaxed, I took our runners packet and read what I should have read sooner, that this course was going to be tough. Thanks. I had already seen that. I would make it anyway.

The Run

Before we started I met a runner, Layne, from Milwaukee, who was in another group. He was running a marathon in every continent. Imagine the traveling. He said that for Antarctica they had to run 400–plus laps around the cruise ship's deck instead, because the weather was too poor to dock. Layne and I stayed in touch during this marathon chase. He turned out to be more of an inspiration to me than he will ever know. Another man said he was in the process of setting a record for the most marathons run in a year wearing sandals, Tom "Hi Guy" Matti. He had just run in Mississippi the day before. Not even 24 hours to train and rest. A third man, Eugene DeFronzo, was just about to complete all 50 for the second time. Eugene would complete the circuit two more times before I finished my first time. With all the obstacles I had to overcome in doing one set of 50, I felt proud enough. I was not going to try for a second time, nor to run all continents. Just get me over those hills.

Eugene told me they made this course one of the toughest of all. Of course, I had to ask him what the toughest one was.

He said, "Pikes Peak." Hmmm.

"Maybe I'll try that one some day," I thought. Anyway, I certainly wasn't going home now. I was going to run. The temperature at 6 a.m. was a humid 70 degrees, a perfect day if I weren't running. I did a couple of warm–up sprints, sweating profusely just over those short trots. My shirt was drenched even before I began. There were fewer participants than I'd ever seen, only 154. Now I could start toward the front. When the gun went off, I began to run a steady clip. After a couple of hundred feet, there was only one runner in front of me. The first mile was downhill. Then, on the second, I met the first steep incline. Slowly, but surely, I made my way up. Nobody passed me until just before mile two. I couldn't believe I had gone so far in second place. After that, only 12 people passed me in the next 20 miles. I must be doing something right.

Mile 11 was along the Missouri River, and I took time to admire it while running. Then I was at Easley Hill, the steepest. I kept telling myself I *could* make it, like the *Little Engine That Could.* Sure enough, I found myself at the top, looking down. That was a great feeling. Not long afterward I was at the halfway mark with a time of 1:39. I really could make my goal of 3:30 if I kept this up. My legs sent signals of pain, but I ignored them and kept up my sub 8–minute pace. Then, all of a sudden, at mile 22, shock waves of pain hit. My right leg was giving up on me. I stopped and stretched. Then I tried to continue at a softer trot. The rest of me wanted to go on, but when my right foot hit the pavement it sent a strong, weird sensation up my leg and through my body that almost made me fall. There went my time. I slowed to a walk, alternating walking with running. The waves of pain continued even this way. Twenty–two more people passed me. I was bummed, but I decided that my right leg probably gave up due to dehydration. If this were true, I could certainly prevent it in the next marathon.

Around the 25th mile I passed the hotel where we were staying, and I saw Jeanne and the kids walking toward the finish line. Even with all the pain, I was still under four hours, not at the goal I had wanted, but I met another goal. I found out that, for the first time, no female had finished in front of me. (OK, I do have just a slight bit of chauvinism in me.)

Time: 3:48:19

17

Visiting Friends
October 21, 2001

KENTUCKY 329 miles

After the hills, I was glad for the mostly flat run of Kentucky. I had done a little training—three nine–mile runs and a couple of six–minute cardio runs—at least that was something. I was as ready as I could be, considering the long hours of work I put in. We stopped in Ohio on the way, to stay a night with Jeanne's parents. It's always good for Austin and Erin to connect with another generation. I tried to make myself useful by cleaning the gutters. Then we all sat down to some home cooking, with the company as warm as the stew.

On Friday, we drove toward Kentucky. We made a short detour to Indiana, where we passed the first home Jeanne and I had shared as newlyweds in Lawrenceburg, before moving to

Hawaii. That house held many sweet memories of a young couple before all the challenges, before I even thought of a marathon. She reached and took my hand and kissed it, remembering. It was comforting to know in every cell of my mind that Jeanne was, and always will be, my girlfriend for life. Not only is she still as beautiful as when I met her, but she holds all of our lives together.

Once in Kentucky, as we were approaching Louisville, we passed farms with race horses. Erin lit up as she saw her favorite animals. "Look, Dad. Horses. Can I ride them, please?" "I'm sorry, sweetheart; these horses have special riders," Jeanne had to tell her. Those well–trained horses behind white fences on manicured, almost blue grass, were waiting to run their own marathons. In Louisville, we stayed, again, with our friends we had known in Hawaii. The kids soon discovered the trampoline, and the four were bouncing through the air, while I helped Bryan paint his deck and the ladies caught up on news. Later on, we all reminisced about the time when we lived in Hawaii, when Bryan and I surprised our wives. We secretly arranged babysitting for the kids, made a home–cooked roast and served it by candle light, and then took the ladies out to see the play, "Cats." Oh, what fun it had been!

The Run

As I waited near the starting line, my old doubts came in. Why on earth was I doing this? I hate to run. I should have trained more. Maybe I should just go back to Jeanne and the kids and say I'd done enough marathons already. But I remembered why I started, to set them an example of working on something, and to keep myself in good physical shape to better care for them. Those things were still truths, so I set my mind in the running mode and did a few sprints. While I was battling pessimistic thoughts, I overheard another runner bragging, "I just love to run. My *whole life* is about running." I wanted to punch him in the nose and tell him to shut up. It was early, 8a.m., on a beautiful day, neither too hot nor cold. The course, I had heard, was pretty, through downtown Louisville and by the Ohio River. I put myself on auto pilot. Another marathon was beginning at the sound of the gun. One mile and then another mile. That's how I always ran. I had gained four pounds, so I set my goal time at 3:45, but I was hoping for 3:30. I ran a couple of miles in seven minutes each. Good. Just keep it up. But at 19 miles, I could feel my legs. They were starting the lactic acid build–up. Now my miles were nine minutes each, and the last one, 11. I saw Jeanne and Barbara and pushed myself across. I was number 40 of 251. Now, at the end, as always, I was very glad I had run. I was also glad we'd made the trip.

Time: 3:34:00

18

Hershey Land
November 11, 2001

PENNSYLVANIA 691 miles

I hadn't planned this run, but I wanted to get in one more before the end of 2001. I looked for the next run listed on the internet. Pennsylvania had one coming up, but scheduling would be a real challenge. To get the time off, I had to trade days with my colleagues. To sweeten the deal, I offered to work two days in exchange for one of them working one. My friends have been a help in making these marathons possible.

It all worked out, and Pennsylvania turned out to be a good next choice. My Aunt Judy, mom's sister, and Uncle Raymond lived nearby. They were happy to drive over. At the end of the race, they were there with Jeanne and the kids, giving me an extra cheering squad. I took them all out to dinner. The other bright spot to the state was the world of chocolate, Hershey, Pennsylvania. The large rides were closed, since we arrived in late autumn, but, unlike Wally World, there was still plenty to do, including driving bumper cars. We rode a ride that passes through a simulated chocolate factory and saw everything that happens between the chocolate bean and the sweet bar: history and geography in a delicious package. Best of all, we received free chocolates at the end of the ride. The kids and I rode the ride three times and then we hit the restaurant and gift shop for even more treats. Then it was back to Harrisburg. That was a pretty capital city, even in late autumn, so clean and neat. The Susquehanna

River flows right through, and there are plenty of parks, including one on an island in the middle of the river. We drove around in the rental car and hoped to tour the capitol, but increased security had canceled tours, so we just shot photos of the outside.

The Run

The starting line was right in front of the capitol. I was chilled and again wishing I had trained more. When would there ever be enough hours in a day? The course was a scenic one, following the river. However, because it was by a river, the winds were fierce. I had to work much harder just to keep my regular pace against the wind. Most of the course was flat, with just a few inclines, especially a steep one at mile 19, at Wildwood Park. By the time I was up and over that one, I was whipped. The rest of the run I had to go a slower pace. I wasn't going to break 3:30, I had to concede. However, they had a very nice medal waiting for me at the end, along with my supporters. So, although I was a tad over the 3:30, I gave a high rating to Pennsylvania for the beauty of the day, the scenery, the nearby chocolate, the city and the company I kept.

Time: 3:33:51

19

A Race For Ed
January 6, 2002

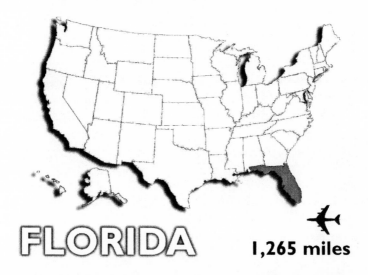

FLORIDA
1,265 miles

For my first run of the new year, I came with a total of four 12–mile runs of training in the freezing cold of a local forest preserve, Busse Woods, in the middle of the night, with a wind chill factor of minus 20. As I had run by moonlight, I saw my freighter plane, the one I usually loaded, flying away from O'Hare, and I was glad that for this night I had not been there working it. The moonlight made the path very visible and easy to follow. I was the only one out there, with the exception of a few scattered animals. Still, the cold and my bad tonsils led me to a bout of strep throat again a week before we left. It was welcoming to arrive to the warmth of Orlando. The town has grown up around Disney World, but not as crowded as Anaheim because Walt made a point of buying extra land to have trees instead of motels nearby. However, we skipped Walt's place in favor of Universal Studios, where we could wander around movie sets. Our favorites were the Terminator 2: 3D and Men In Black sets. We were *in* the movies for a minute. Also, there were visits to the sets of Twister, Earthquake and King Kong. On these trips almost any behavior is accepted, because people pay to be children again, to run, yell, and act a little crazy. It's worth every cent to be out of any mold, out of school, out of work. The next day was more of the same on the rides of Islands of Adventure. The only drawback is that once inside, you have to eat what they sell, which is always over–priced, but delicious.

The Run

I arrived at this run earlier than any other due to some rowdy people in our hotel who made sleeping impossible. I decided I'd drive to the starting area, arriving near the site at a dark 1a.m. We were going to run inside Disney World itself, with all the attractions around us. Already there were people setting up signs and tables for water. Five more hours to go.

Trying to get some rest, I left the car and heater on and played soft music on the radio. I reclined the seat and went into a state of almost sleep with the words of the songs floating by. After what seemed like only an hour, I heard voices all around me. Actually, it was 3:15 a.m. The first buses of runners had arrived. I turned off the car and tried to go back to that state of almost sleep, but the people were making more and more noise as they stretched and leaned against cars waiting.

By 4 a.m. there were thousands around me. Then, a few minutes later, they suddenly disappeared. I got out to find a porta–potty and asked someone where everyone went. That's when I found out I had-n't set my watch forward. It was already 5:30 in Florida. I had to hurry to the starting line a half mile away. The run had an atmos-phere of fun from the beginning. Mickey and Minnie were there, along with many of their friends. There was a fireworks display right after the starting gun. Cool. I was fired up and ready to go. Because of the crowds it took a full minute just to cross the actual starting line. It took another three or four minutes to get away from the throngs and be able to run at my pace. I moved along, enjoying being there, when…oh, no. An awful stitch on my right side. I had to slow down, hoping I wouldn't have to stop. My last two marathons were nonstoppers, and I wanted this to be, too. Side stitches are painful, and they take your breath away. I tried breathing techniques that are supposed to help, along with a slower pace to run through this, but the damn thing wouldn't go away. It still hurt at two miles and five miles and nine miles.

By the 12th mile, I knew if I was able to complete the race at all, my time would not be great. At the halfway mark, I was just under two hours. Not good. Despite all the pain, I was still aware of the scenery. We ran through all the theme parks. Disney characters waved and called, "Good job. Keep it up!" as we passed. That gave me a great push. However, by the 14th mile the lactate in my legs was beginning to affect me, to give me "the burn." On the plus side, the stitch in my side was gone. Too late. I didn't have the inner force to pick up my pace now. I just had to grind it out, taking pleasure in the run through Cinderella's castle that I had seen so often on TV. Then it was out into the open again, where the sky greeted us with a torrent of rain. The rest of the run was wet. Pain, lactate and rain, combined with, perhaps, not enough training, brought me to the finish after four hours. But I had made it. I had not stopped. Every time it seems a small miracle that I am able to complete another marathon. I thought I might actually make this 50 & D.C.

Time: 4:06:50

Due to logistics, Jeanne and the kids could not meet me at the finish, but I soon found them at our agreed-upon spot. Despite my soaking wet shirt, I received my usual warm reception. There was one more treat in Florida. After I had showered, we headed up the coast to Daytona to visit Jeanne's brother Ed, a man full of fun, who reminded me of the actor Sam Elliot. Ed took us to the Daytona 500 speedway for a tour. The noise of the passing cars was almost deafening, but that added to the excitement. After the tour, he and his girlfriend ordered pizza, and we all watched the

Chicago Bears dominate the Jacksonville Jaguars 33 to 13. We all had fun, never imagining it would be the last time we would ever see Ed. Tragically, he passed away in late September of that year at only 39. His ashes were scattered over the Daytona speedway and the Atlantic Ocean. It was a blessing that we ended our Florida trip with a stop to visit him.

20

The Lonely Trip
February 17, 2002

LOUISIANA ✈ 1,070 miles

This trip began with a disappointment. We had been planning it for several months already. We were going to rent a car and drive across the world's longest bridge, go on a swamp tour, visit a voodoo museum, and see the street acts. The flight was scheduled for 6 a.m., Saturday morning. We got up at 3:30 a.m. so we could leave home by 4. Everything was packed and in the van for the ride to the airport. Since it was only a couple of days past our anniversary, I reasoned that the cost of this trip was why I couldn't replace that diamond. Jeanne, without fail, reminds me of the diamond every February. Then we heard Austin. He was stumbling, trying to make it to the bathroom, but he was sick all over the rug. Poor kid. We helped him clean up and gave him some water and waited a few minutes. Maybe it would all be over with that and he'd still be able to travel. No such luck. He said he couldn't even ride to the airport, much less make a trip. He was very ill. We helped him lie back down and put a cool rag on his forehead. It was clear he wasn't going anywhere. This was tough. They had always gone with me, but the hotel and the marathon were already paid. Jeanne agreed I should go on alone, although my heart wasn't in it. I went to unpack the van of all the suitcases except mine. Although I work at the airport and make the trip almost every day, this ride was the longest I had made. It was painful to leave my best friends at home. All during the flight I kept missing them, but at least Austin was sick in his own bed and not in a strange place. In my New Orleans hotel, I had run into my friends from Milwaukee whom I had met in Missouri, CJ and Layne. They assured me that I would not have enjoyed the swamp tour; they thought it was a complete two–hour rip–off. Also, when I saw the rowdy crowds in the French Quarter, I realized it wasn't a place to bring kids. Erin would have been bored, Austin would have tolerated it, and Jeanne would have actually liked it. Well, I was there now with my friends, so I was going to enjoy what I could. The weather was a cool 50, without a cloud in the sky. You have to get into the mood of the place. Once I did, I enjoyed myself, and then instead of being depressed, I felt a little guilty. I watched the street entertainers play banjo and fiddle music, with the lively rhythm known only to Louisiana. I was tapping my toes, and some tourists took up dancing in the street. We stopped in a restaurant that was in the courtyard of an old brick building and had bowls of shrimp gumbo. I was then fully initiated into New Orleans. Mardi Gras was over already, but the festive atmosphere continued.

The Run

Sunday Morning I found Layne at the starting line where everyone seemed to be in a very festive mood. I was nervous, but not as much as usual. Maybe I was finally getting used to these runs. I had a good pace as we went through the French Quarter and then down a park area. There was only one small incline, over a bridge, and then it was all flat. I could do this one in 3:30 easily, I decided. I did the first 16 miles in two hours. This pace would work. Then it happened. Around the 18th mile, I started feeling the "burn." It progressed quickly, and by mile 22, I had slowed down significantly. By mile 24

I had to admit the idea of 3:30 was out the window. When your legs don't work well, there's nothing you can do but just grind it out the best you can, so that's what I did. I was able to just keep going and make it across the finish line, although I was looking for the faces that weren't there. At least I was proud that I had a fourth nonstopper in a row. I hadn't even stopped with "the burn." With thanks, I accepted the medal that came with a lavender bead necklace. My time wasn't that far off my goal, despite what happened, and the scenery was great. I sat down to stretch my sore legs, missing the stretching by Jeanne.

Time: 3:36:16

I didn't want to stay there thinking of that anymore. I had the free beer offered and went to the hotel to clean up and then back to Bourbon Street. There, Dick Grayson and the Goat Dirt Road Band livened the afternoon air with dancing tunes. I watched talented mimes, painters and magicians draw crowds around themselves. Then I looked for a place with live music that wasn't a bar. I found it—Cajun Cabin. The sounds were fun and the jambalaya and alligator bits delicious. After that, I wandered the street as part of the tourist flow and ran into some other runners who were also working on their 50 states. This was a nice group to hang with. I was becoming more determined in my goals, and actually glad I was one of them now. For a few minutes, out of curiosity, I went into a nude lady bar. Admission was free, but you had to buy a beer. One of the dancers came on to me and started a more friendly conversation than I wanted. I told her I was happily married and, giving her five dollars and my beer, I left. My mind was now on those waiting for me at home. I was ready to fly. On the flight I looked out the window at the oil wells speckling the Gulf of Mexico. They seemed tall, even from 28,000 feet. I waved down at Louisiana. It had turned out all right after all. Now I wanted a run with the family again.

21

Almost Without Them
March 24, 2002

WASHINGTON, D.C. 732 miles

For this trip we headed to the airport talking of the monuments and museums we were going to see in the capital. However, when they announced "Keesler" and we went running to the counter there was only one open seat, not four.

"Okay, I'm not going then," I announced, but Jeanne encouraged me to take the ticket. She assured me that she and the kids would get another flight later that day.

On that note, I reluctantly boarded the plane, so rushed I forgot to leave Jeanne the van keys. Again, I was as depressed as I had been on the trip to New Orleans. These vacations were supposed to be family affairs. As soon as my plane landed in Newark, I called a coworker in Chicago who connected me with Jeanne. "I'm sorry, Marlin, but we aren't going to make it out today."

"I'm coming back." "You don't want to do that, honey. Everything is pre–paid. Go ahead. I'm sure we'll get a flight tomorrow," she insisted.

I finally gave in and told her to call as soon as she heard anything. Luckily, one of my coworkers gave them a ride home. We're a close group at the airlines. On the next flight, I closed my eyes and imagined they were with me. Then I smiled, remembering the night before. We had not left then because we went to watch Austin play in an indoor soccer game with the special ed team. He was so proud to be out with a group running up and down the floor. For a few minutes, his lack of social skills and "common sense" didn't matter; he was a player. Our son was a soccer player. Remembering his grin as he came off the floor tired and sweaty with the other guys, I knew it was worth starting a day late and being on separate flights. They'd surely be there tomorrow. Remembering helped. Before I knew it, I was in D.C. and on my way to the hotel. As soon as I checked in, I rushed to the marathon registration. If I was late, I wouldn't be allowed to run. I was surprised to find a full airport–like security check–in. Runners had to open bags and walk through a metal detector. It seemed a shame that society had come to this stage, but I eventually had my packet and was on my way. That night was like all my pre–marathon nights, tossing and turning and anticipation jitters. I wished I had run more in the weeks before. I wished my right leg were not sore. Then I fell asleep and dreamed the usual dream, that I had overslept and missed the race.

The Run

Actually, rather than being late, I was at the starting area two hours early, freezing in my short sleeved T–shirt and shorts. I looked around at the other runners, who were all bundled up. Did they know more in advance than I did? This race should be later in the year. Then the sun rose over the Potomac River, producing an awe-inspiring moment. No, this was the right day and time to be here. I enjoyed the tranquility. The gun went off at 7 a.m. and I was on my way. It was mostly a decline, so I made the first mile in 7 minutes. Good. Between the second and third mile, I encountered my first hill and my right leg was beginning to bother me. I started my same old refrain: Why am I doing this? I just kept going, running through the pain, focusing on making each mile 8 minutes or less.

When I run, I carry on a mental conversation with Jeanne, envisioning her at the finish. Even though she had not made it Sunday, but was certainly going to make it for sightseeing the next day, I still mentally spoke as if she were there. At each mile I told her where I was and assured her (and myself) that it wasn't going to be much longer. Although I was working hard, I had to admit I was also having a good run. Even with a steep hill at mile 6, I breezed through it. I started to enjoy the course, passing monuments and memorials. I didn't get the burn in my legs until the 20th mile, but there was a decline, and as I ran down, I actually passed a couple of people. I was able to finish in my second best time and my fifth nonstopper in a row. Perhaps I was getting used to the runs, pain and all.

Time: 3:26:49

I do like crossing the finish line and accepting the medal. It makes it all worth while. I thanked them for my D.C. medal and ran to call Jeanne. She and the kids had been bumped off flights for two days now. Working for an airline might seem glamorous at times, but I'm here to tell you that flying standby really sucks. Although they would arrive late, they would eventually make it to D.C. On the subway ride back, I gloated a little, wearing my medal around my neck. I went back to rest before playing tour guide on Monday. As soon as they arrived, we went right to George Washington's Mount Vernon Estate & Gardens, as I talked to the kids about the man on the one–dollar bill. Riding through Alexandria, I was surprised to see so much red brick. They were in every building. Once at Washington's home, we ate in a little colonial restaurant, taking in the flavors of the past, before taking the tour. On Tuesday, Lincoln, on the five–dollar bill, was waiting for us in his gigantic stone chair. We looked tiny as we posed for the touristy photo below him. I gave the kids a brief "out of school" history lesson on the man. Then we had a more solemn moment as we visited the Vietnam Memorial. There, engraved in granite, were over 58,000 names of American soldiers who made the ultimate sacrifice during the Vietnam conflict. Using paper and pencil, I scratched off 2 names, that of Lance Sijan, who died a POW and had a book written about him ("Into the Mouth of the Cat"), and that of Stephen Keesler. I hope to research this man with my name.

From there we went by the Washington Monument, with its top reaching the low clouds in the sky on this rainy day, but we didn't go in. We chose instead the Air and Space Museum of the Smithsonian Institute. Working around airplanes every day, I am still impressed by them, especially the tiny one, The Spirit of St. Louis, in which Charles Lindberg dared to cross the Atlantic. Then Jeanne had to rush to the airport to be back in time for work. The kids and I saw the White House from a distance, but they were tired and ready to go back and play around in the hotel's pool. There's a limit on sight-seeing with kids. By Wednesday, Austin was sick again and just want-ed to "chill," while Erin and I went to Arlington Cemetery in search of soldiers. We found the Tomb of the Unknown Soldier. We wit-nessed the changing of the guard and watched soldiers in a passing funeral parade with a riderless horse. We had found them. I was glad I had read so much about our capital's history before the trip, so I could give my little speeches at each sight. Maybe some of what I told the kids will be remembered, but in any case, being in those places will never be forgotten. It was good that I added D.C. to the state-a-thon. What made it even more special is that the D.C. marathon organization went bankrupt, and this was the only all–D.C. marathon ever held.

22

The Shivering Idiot
April 28, 2002

NEW JERSEY   866 miles

I can't believe I ran this one. I did it just to get another state checked off my list. Since D.C., I had only run one nine–miler and two attempted nine–milers for training. I had a stack of excuses for not running more. There were always excuses. My family and work always come first. That would cover at least 50% of why I didn't put more miles on my shoes. The other 50% can be chalked up to my lack of desire to run in Illinois snow and rain in the middle of the night. Maybe I just had a greater desire to spend more time with the family watching TV on the couch. Or, possibly, I'm just lazy? Whatever the reasons, I wasn't really up to this run. I watched the entry deadline draw closer and closer over the internet. The run would close at 2,000 entrants. Three weeks prior to the run, entries had reached 1,900. At that point I was still unsure. (I had actually paid to run this marathon twice before and could not get off work.) Finally, I decided this run's time had come. I sent in my money.

Maybe I'd have work conflicts again. No. There was a little block of time between my Saturday morning shift and my Sunday night one. A run would just fit. My body was still complaining, but efficient Jeanne made all the reservations for car rental and hotel just in case. I tried to persuade her to bring the kids and come, too, but the time was so cramped, I had no luck. I went to bed at 10 p.m. Friday night still unprepared, but at 12:30 a.m. I was wide awake. I got up, packed and listed myself on a flight. I was at work by 4 a.m. There was no excuse not to go, and it was pouring rain all day. Maybe it would be good to get away. I was off work at 2 p.m. and on the flight at 3 p.m. I landed on a beautiful afternoon in Newark and dashed to Dollar for my rental. Then I met the New Jersey freeways. Construction had me so lost I ended up going north instead of south. No problem. Just turn around, right? Actually, I found myself somehow in a rush of speeding cars on the Garden State Parkway, with toll booths asking for money. The construction I had just driven out of had me in the "Exact Change Only" lane. I couldn't get over without causing an accident, and I wasn't going to throw in a dollar bill, so I kept going. Because I had slowed down trying to figure out what to do, other cars behind were honking. At the next booth down the highway, the lady said not to worry about missing the toll, so I didn't worry. Friendly state. I just kept driving and trying to find Edison. By 8 p.m., after having seen more of New Jersey than I ever wanted, I finally found my hotel. After some spaghetti at a nearby restaurant, I returned to the hotel and reviewed the marathon information packet. I quickly realized that the marathon started at 9 a.m. instead of 8 a.m. This might cause some problems catching my return flight. That worry made for another restless night of sleep.

A short few hours later, I was up and hoping that this day would go a little better. It didn't. It was worse. There was a heavy, windy rain that blocked almost all my view, and I barely saw the road signs. Result: I was headed southwest instead of southeast. This marathon was point to point, which meant I had to catch a bus from the finish area to the start area. The literature stated the last bus left at 6 a.m. sharp. I instantly found myself with two problems. It was 5:30 a.m. and I was going the wrong way, and I had to use the bathroom something terrible. I pulled over and studied the map, finding a route that would take me east then back north to where I needed to be. I was quickly running out of time, while at the same time trying to keep my bladder from bursting. When I decided that I could absolutely wait no longer I took the next exit ramp. Then, quite by accident, I stopped in a hotel to use the facilities and saw there were other runners just like me. They were waiting for the last bus to the starting line. After a relieving trip to the facilities, I grabbed my stuff and followed them. At 6:45 I stepped off the bus into a freezing downpour. I could easily have gotten back on for a ride back, but the bus wasn't budging, so I kept walking. On the beach were a couple of porta–potties, a concession stand and a makeshift canvass tent, with over a thousand people crowded in, trying to stay dry. I was wearing soaked sweat pants and my long–sleeved Louisville marathon sweatshirt. I grabbed a plastic garbage bag for a raincoat and shivered uncontrollably with the others. The water was running downhill into the floor of the tent, so we might as well have been in a river. As teenagers say, I thought, "This sucks!" The only thing my brain could process for the two hours of waiting was, "Idiot. Idiot. Idiot. Idiot!" Oh, man! I couldn't believe I was doing this. "I'm an idiot." It was horrible. Just then, an administrator announced that there was a bus to take back those who decided not to make the run. Escape was waiting for me right inside that bus, and a trip to warmth, blessed warmth. I looked around at the others. Several of them shouted out, "Booo!" They were conspiring against me. As much as I wanted to, I wasn't going to humiliate myself by leaving now. I *would* run.

Well, if I was going to do it, it couldn't be in these heavy clothes. I did a superman act and changed into running shorts and a tank top in a cramped porta–potty.

The Run

At the starting point, I saw that thousands were still over–dressed. I also noticed that the rain was slowing a little. Okay, I'd give it a try. On the first five miles, despite everything, I wasn't doing that bad, taking about 7:20 minutes a mile; better than I expected. It rained during the entire run, but not nearly as hard as it had beforehand. We still had to run through puddles. This run had time pacers, runners with expected finishing times written on the backs of their shirts, and I was able to keep up with the 3:20 pacer. I was doing okay. There was a small side pain, but I ran through it. Just past mile 20, a runner going the other way called out my number. He was one of the guys I'd met in the New Orleans run. Cool. Someone recognized me.

Encouraged by the thought, I tried to speed up, but my legs had no more to give and were slowing down. I just felt good to cross the finish line and get this one over. Actually, on the other side of the line, I was pleased with myself that I had stuck it out. Another state to add and my sixth nonstopper in a row. It was also another marathon without my team at the finish line. However, considering the soggy mess, I was glad, in a way, they hadn't made the trip.

Time: 3:45:29

The excitement wasn't over yet. That hour delay for the start caused me to miss my flight back. The next flight was cancelled. I had to get back to work, and if I didn't make it, there would be consequences. The last flight had one open seat left. I'm not sure what made me happier, finishing the marathon or getting that last seat as an airline employee traveling standby.

Being alone in New Jersey, there was no point in visiting the nearby casinos. I just looked out at the waves of the Atlantic, bought some saltwater taffy and fudge in boxes with drawings of the ocean on them as souvenirs and headed home. For Washington State, I would definitely have the family back again as cheerleaders and fellow sightseers. New Jersey had one more souvenir for me. Dollar Rent A Car sent me nice little photo of myself passing through the toll booth without paying. There was also an equally nice note saying my credit card had been charged $25 to pay the fine. Greetings from the Garden State.

23

Lots To See and Do
May 19, 2002

WASHINGTON 2,108 miles

This was one of our better planned vacations. We had time to enjoy the view and eat the most expensive meal of our lives atop the Space Needle in Seattle. But before all that came the pre–run training. I really am not motivated before a run, but I decided to substitute focus for motivation. If I could just stay focused for training runs, beyond family and work, someday I might make the required time necessary to qualify for Boston. Okay, I would do it. I bought myself a new pair of running shoes to help my focus. I was pumped up in these. I was healthy at this time, too, so that really helped. I was sure I could break a new personal record in Olympia.

So I set off to train. The weather was perfect; I had no job conflicts. I was pumped up and did a good nine mile run. This was working. I'd do it again. The next time I went out training, almost as soon as I started, I felt really weird pains in and throughout both legs. I've had pain before on training runs, but when I got going, the circulation of blood got rid of it. Not this time. This time it was like hundreds of weak sensations were pulsating all over. Every time one of my feet landed, it was like flashing strobe lights emitting charges of pain instead of light. I slowed down and then tried to just walk. The pain was there just the same. I could hardly wait to get home and off my feet. I had a bad case of shin splints that I believe were caused by the wrong kind of new shoes. For the next 10 days it was the same. Like with Las Vegas, everything for Olympia was pre–paid. That encouraged me to go and at least try, but also I didn't want to have a DNF (did not finish). I thought about it over and over and, as usual, I finally decided we should go. We had not all been to a run for a while, and we could at least enjoy the trip.

The Run

The day was ready to cooperate, a cool 45 with only a light drizzle. But my legs? Before the run I did something I usually don't do, I took two Advil. The night before Jeanne had given my legs a good massage. I arrived at the starting line and did my usual sprints and stretches and waited. A miracle. No pain. Zilch. Nada. I might actually make it. I was ready for the horn, and before it went off, I happened to see a runner in the crowd with a New Jersey Shore finisher's shirt. A fellow sufferer of the deluge. There was no time to go over and talk rain stories, though. The run was about to start.

The horn went off at 7:30 sharp, and we were on our way. My breathing was a little hard up and down the small hills of the first five miles, but then I found I could maintain a good pace. I worried about my legs the whole time. When is the pain going to come back? It never did. My legs felt some soreness and were heavier than usual, but that dreaded pain from Chicago stayed gone. By mile 23, my breathing was smooth enough to carry on a conversation with a fellow runner. Then I looked at my watch and saw I had 9 minutes and 2 seconds to reach my goal of breaking 3:30. I reached deep down inside and gave it all I had down the last hill. Close, but no cigar. But that didn't matter when Erin came out to greet me, touching my thumb in our traditional family bonding. My crew was there. That made it a good run.

Time: 3:30:20

Later, at the aquarium, when I heard Erin laugh as she looked through the glass at the shark, who might have been looking back at her, I knew it was a good vacation. Austin was waving at the sting rays and colored fish. If I didn't have the deadlines of the marathons, I'd never do all the juggling of schedules at work to travel to so many places. We'd be lucky to see 50 states in 50 years of vacations. As it was, here I was driving to Seattle from Olympia in a rental car to go up the Space Needle. On the ride up, I held on tightly, trying to ignore my fear of heights I'd had since I was a boy hanging tobacco. However, once at the top, the view of the city and the snow–topped Mount Rainier around it was worth any trepidation I had felt.

Safely back on firm ground, I took them to see several fields of Weyerhaeuser tree farms. Each field displayed trees at different stages of growth. I explained how the trees are harvested, and we talked about all of the things that are created from wood. Next we said "Hi" to the monarch and the hundreds of other species of butterflies in the zoo. They have their own marathon, flying up from Mexico every year, a mileage that beats my 50-state total. My favorite stop was at the Boeing 747 plant in Renton. This is the aircraft I work on at night. My whole family has been to work with me at one time or

another, so we were all interested in the tour, which showed us the assembly of one of the world's largest aircraft from beginning to end. For both the run and the sightseeing, I was glad my legs had cooperated for Washington.

24

A Family Affair
June 8, 2002

INDIANA   127 miles

To add a little fun to this trip, while we were at the Runners' Expo, Jeanne and the kids signed up to do the 5K walk. Now we were all in the exercise program. The expo also had a stage with music blasting through the hall, and Erin jumped up to join the children dancing. We were off to a good start. The expos give you a feeling you're part of a great club. I even met a 53–year–old lady who said she had made a 3:03 finish on her last run in Kentucky. This is certainly a sport for a lifetime. By the time we had seen the expo and checked in, it was 9 p.m., and we hadn't eaten since lunch. I have a rule, instilled by the Michigan experience, that I won't eat 12 hours or less before a run. Throwing the rule book out the window, I took us all to fill up on spaghetti. Then it was back to the hotel, where all of us went straight to bed. The kids were in a bed across from us. About 10 minutes later, when I was half–asleep, on the edge of La La Land, Jeanne and I heard whispers. Turning to their bed, we saw Austin and Erin sitting upright, staring at us in some kind of anticipation. (Gee, have we reached that time in life to give one of those talks?) We told them to lie back down and go to sleep. I needed to get a little sleep.

The Run

Actually, I was up early for the run, which began at the College Football Hall of Fame. I was off to a good start, making the first mile in 6 minutes and 15 seconds. I thought maybe the marker was misplaced. It didn't feel like I ran that fast. After that, the times went up to 7, but I kept them below an eight. I was able to make the halfway mark in 1:41:37. Good. Then the spaghetti I should not have eaten started sending me signals. After some distance of running with "squeezed cheek syndrome" I had to make a pit stop in the porta–potty. That ended my streak of nonstop marathons. Disappointment, but I kept moving forward. During the second half, I found myself running beside a lady who was in her late 40s and running the half–marathon. She stopped for the water tables, so I did, too. It was hot, and my legs were getting heavy. I figured it was already too late to make the goal time. She told me she had run

Boston in the spring. Boston; that was on my list of "some days."
Amazingly. she said she had eight children and didn't even *start* running until they were grown. She must have trained well once she
started because she moved on ahead of me. As I kept going, the
course went through a park, and I lost sight of the runner ahead of
me. Fortunately, the ground was marked, so I was able to stay on
track. I heard later that several lead runners had been misdirected and
taken an extra mile by mistake. I followed the markers and found
myself inside the Notre Dame Stadium crossing the finish line, which
was also the 50–yard line.

Time: 3:44:45

In the stadium, Jeanne and the kids were waiting, the best part
of any run. It turned out to be a blessing that I had such a poor time.
It put me there just as they had completed their 5K walk, tired, but
grinning that they had made their own run, too. We all had finisher
T–shirts.

After showers, we came back to tour the Notre Dame campus.
The Basilica of the Sacred Heart was breathtaking inside and gave us
a quiet pause in the day before visiting the campus. On this trip we
were all winners.

25

Elvis Territory
September 1, 2002

MISSISSIPPI   691 miles

We were able to make this run thanks to Jeanne's ability to plan. It was almost Labor Day, and our other holiday plans had fallen through. We were going to have three full days with nothing to do, a rarity. So on Monday night, August 26th, while I was at work, Jeanne was checking a list of Labor Day weekend runs and started making reservations. Mississippi, here we come. We started driving at 6 p.m. Friday afternoon and pulled into Tupelo the next afternoon. I went to get my runner's packet, which included a cool shirt, orange, with a skull and crossbones. Then we took a tour of the course. A few hills, but nothing to bad. It was time for a Bonanza dinner.

Back at the hotel, the kids chose their favorite sight of all the trips, the swimming pool. In pools, they cool off and are just themselves, with a little swimming, but much more yelling and making cannonball jumps. Jeanne patiently watched them at a dry distance, while I went to the store for foot cushions. When I came back, I was waving at them in the pool when I felt a sudden sharp pain. Oh, my gosh! What happened? I was just stung by a wasp and the little bugger got away with it. The nerve of that insect! But I wasn't going to be stopped. I went to lie down and, by 3:30 a.m., I was awake and raring to go. This time they woke up with me, so we all headed, sleepy–eyed in the pre–dawn dark, for the starting point. As I was waiting for the start, Austin asked me a highly cognitive question. "What do you think of while you run?"

Lots of people have asked me that question, but it meant more coming from him. I told him it was a secret that I'd share someday. He accepted that and waited with me in the almost silent dark. The only sounds were those of crickets chirping in a far–off wood.

The Run

The silence was broken by, "On your marks. Get set. GO!" I was running, but out of breath for the first five miles. My weight was back up to 170, and I really felt it. I accepted the fact that this was not going to be one of my best performances. I had done training runs at night, and it's very similar to a dark marathon, except here there are silhouetted shapes running ahead of me that my mind could turn into almost anything it wants. Also, running in the open field at night where I train is different from running in thick woods. The sounds in an open field are distant, and I feel freer. However, while going through the woods at night, the sounds echo off the vegetation and are louder. That gives a spooky, compressed feeling. But in both places, running at night gives much more adrenaline, so I rushed on.

It was light enough to see my watch at the 9–mile mark, and I also saw my first armadillo. By the 11th mile, the sun came up, and I was feeling all right. Between miles 21 and 22 I had the pleasant surprise of looking up to see Jeanne and the kids waiting with a bottle of Gatorade, cheering me on. My three. Just what I needed. They also showed up at miles 24 and 25 for an added boost. I didn't break any records, but I had done another nonstopper. That felt good. Now to see Tupelo.

Time: 3:48:03

This is a town that will never let you forget that Elvis was born there. We saw the small, white wooden home where he was born and posed with a statue of him at age 13. Then we drove up to Memphis, covering the miles he had covered as a starting singer. On the way, we stopped by a cotton field, so the kids could pick some and see where it all comes from. Coming into Memphis we passed the FedEx hub at the airport, but we headed on straight for Graceland. It's like a 1970s time capsule. It had green shag carpeting on the ceiling. We weren't allowed to take photos inside, but we took some by his automobile and jet collection. He had certainly gone a long way in his change of homes, but they say his heart was always with his mom. He is buried next to her, his father, grandmother and twin brother, who died at birth. His music is buried in the hearts of people around the world. He sang in many languages, from Hawaiian to German. I had heard his Wedding Song in Hawaii, not knowing I'd someday be in his home.

After the home, we'd had enough of being tourists. We set out for a campground and a marshmallow roast over an open fire. The kids loved that and the singing, but after an hour in the hot, humid tent, they were asking, "Can we find a hotel. I want air conditioning," and "I want a pool."

So much for the great outdoors. The next run was going to be cooler: a mile high.

26

Up, Up, and Away
September 8, 2002

NEW MEXICO 1,358 miles

Way up in Albuquerque, 5,500 feet high, we went up even higher, in one of the colorful hot air balloons. We were able to help unpack the balloon and watch the burners being lit. Then we climbed in and started skyward. The view of the valley and surrounding mountains was spectacular. We all loved the ride except for Erin, who was bothered by the noise of the burners. She had her fingers in her ears and tears in her eyes for most of the trip. When we came down, the balloon pilot of Sweet Escapes treated us to a picnic lunch and wine for the adults. Erin, now on quieter ground, reinforced the fact that she had a terrible experience. I only wished I had brought earplugs from work so she would have had the same thrilling ride the rest of us had.

After the airborne trip, we were psyched up for more sights, so we set out for the Petroglyph National Monument, where we climbed over rocks that had had drawings of animals and cool designs carved into them by Native Americans over a thousand years ago. I wondered what kind of life the people who carved these petroglyphs had had. For sure, they ran miles over this land, as I was about to do.

We also took a ride on the world's longest tram to Sandia Peak, where we enjoyed a panoramic view of Albuquerque while eating at a restaurant on top.

The Run

Jeanne was up early to drive me to the marathon bus that took runners to the starting area. I was actually a little over–confident for this one, since the race director described it as downhill for eleven miles of the course. Easy. I started off with this confidence, but I was very winded for the first mile. What was the matter? Then I realized I hadn't counted on the effect of being up so high. I'd have to really work on this one after all. It was still dark, but without the noises of Mississippi, just almost black and quiet. I kept moving forward. By the eighth mile, I had sunlight and was going downhill. Maybe I could do all right anyway, despite the elevation and a strong headwind as we ran bellow Sandia Peak. I was wrong. By the 12th mile, the altitude really started to take its toll. I was running a mile in *nine* minutes. My legs were tight and my thighs were killing me. I was breathing well, but getting less oxygen. This was causing a quicker lactic acid buildup in my leg muscles. This was going to be a long run, I had to admit. Add to that the fact that the Mississippi run had been only a week before, and I was running with very little sleep, since I worked all Thursday night. I just was not going to make good time.

Once I accepted this, I relaxed and started to enjoy the view, looking down at Albuquerque. It was spectacular scenery, second only to Honolulu. Then I was treated to a rainbow that hung over the city for two hours. I passed a herd of buffalo who just stared at me, probably wondering why I wanted to move so quickly on a lovely day. There was no one chasing me. By mile 22, I had to just walk part of the way. The other runners must have felt the altitude, too, as I came in at number 27 of 103—and I was still under four hours. Now I would forget the struggle to run so high and just enjoy the last part of the vacation with my family.

Time: 3:55:27

While we were in the area, I decided we should see the place where four states meet: Four Corners. You can stand in Utah, Colorado, Arizona and New Mexico, all at the same time. That was a good geography lesson, so it was worth the 200–mile drive.

I headed west and turned north by Shiprock, a tiny town named for the sacred mountain rock of the Navajo. The town had a pizza place for Navajos to stop before taking their multicolored blankets and painted sand art to tourist shops. Beyond that, we drove through their reservation, dotted with hogans (small, round one–room homes) with outhouses, miles from the nearest neighbor.

The scenery on the way north was even bleaker, taller rock mountains with absolutely nothing growing on them. It looked like a scene from the moon. I hoped our car would not give out there. We wouldn't be found for weeks. But I kept going. We *were* going to see the spot with four states.

After four long hours we saw the sign and stopped to pose with it. "Four Corners Monument—Navajoland, U.S.A." However, right after that was a sign reading, "Temporarily Closed." What? We drove four hours to see a closed park? A man in a nearby car said they

closed it because a wind storm the previous night blew down all of the vendor stands. Darn. There was nothing to do but take a few more photos and leave, this time by a more scenic route. On our return, we experienced our own fierce wind that blew tumbleweeds across our path.

Back in Albuquerque, we had one more place to play tourists, Old Town. There, we walked by stores exhibiting art from the cultures of Native America, Spain, Mexico, and the U.S. We chose Mexican for our cuisine, feasting on tacos and warm corn tortillas with butter. We had now savored the state from all angles and were ready to head to South Dakota.

27

A Wonderful Place to Visit
October 13, 2002

SOUTH DAKOTA **882 miles**

As a family excursion, South Dakota was a huge success. We had an absolutely wonderful time. However, I found the marathon to be no more than personal brutality.

Let's begin with the fun stuff. Our first stop was Wall Drug. There, the walls are covered with postcards from all over the world from people who once stopped by there. Outside, Austin posed riding a large, fake buffalo and Jeanne bought some moccasins. I also bought a book, *Undaunted Courage*, about Lewis and Clark. The author, Stephen Ambrose, passed away just a few days after I bought the book, but he tells a great tale of the discoveries of those men. I could relate their travels to those I was having for my marathon quest, overcoming obstacles, although different ones, to make travel possible. As usual, the favorite tourist spot for the kids was the hotel pool.

This one, in Rapid City, had a twisting, turning slide that landed them in the water screaming with joy. I had to slide down it a couple times myself. The next day I pulled them out of the pool long enough to visit Bear Country, a very cool drive–through zoo, where you had to keep the windows rolled up, and you had to wait for the animals to get out of your way. This place was neat. You couldn't get any closer to the animals than we were. We watched a couple of rams bash their heads together, saw a cougar climb a tall tree and waited 10 minutes for the bear to get out of our way. From there we went on to a memorial where sculptors are carving a giant replica of Crazy Horse in stone. It's been 50 years since its inception, and it's expected to take 50 more years to complete. Such patience. I hope to come back in twenty years and see how it's doing. As I took the standard photo of Erin and Austin in front of the small version, I wondered how they'd be doing in 20 years. Would they find work? Would they be able to take care of themselves? I plan for Jeanne and me to be their neighbors, helping out and visiting.

After the Crazy Horse Memorial, we went to one that began much earlier, Mount Rushmore. From their lofty perch, Presidents Lincoln, Washington, Jefferson (my favorite) and Roosevelt, all larger than life, watch over the land forever. I took this opportunity to discuss the contributions each had made to our nation.

We left the presidents for a visit to a nearby cave, where our guide took us down some steep steps and narrow passageways until we came to a large underground room. At this point, he proceeded to explain the history and geology of the cave. There were about ten of us standing there listening to our guide and one little girl carrying on a conversation of her own. When Erin walked into this room, she stopped and looked around and then blurted out, "Oh! This is my house. This is my kitchen and this is my living room." She walked around pointing to different rock objects and describing how they were different pieces of furniture in her home. All of us, except the perturbed guide, thought Erin was cute and comical. The nonverbal actions of the guide indicated that we needed to shut this kid up. So we did, in a gentle way, and moved on. After the cave we went to another place that put a smile on all of our faces. It's called the Cosmos Mystery Area, and it was absolutely worth the stop. It was like the place was from the *Twilight Zone*, it broke all of the rules of gravity. A dropped ball would roll uphill. Standing sideways felt normal. In one particular spot, Erin looked taller than Austin. Simply put, this place was neat.

Next, we went further west, to see a tall, steep mountain, Devil's Tower, in Wyoming. From what little we saw, it looked like the main population of Wyoming was prairie dogs, hundreds standing on their hind legs studying us, running their own marathons across the prairie. "Marathon." Where had I heard that word before? Time to stop touring and start running.

The Run

Describing the run as one of personal brutality is an understatement. Again, I had not prepared as I should have, and boy was I going to pay for it. Jeanne got me to the last bus that takes runners to the start just in time. But on the way our bus broke down about two miles away from the start. It was a sight to behold. There were about 20 male runners on the bus and only one female runner, plus the female bus driver. We were out in the middle of nowhere next to an open field with some horses in it. One guy hurried off the bus and proceeded to relieve himself next to the fence between the bus and the field. Another guy shouted out, "Hey, that's a good idea." The next thing the two females witnessed was a line of 20 guys along the fence, facing away from the bus, all relieving themselves—except one. That was me. I had stage fright, so I faked it. Finally, another bus came by and had us all there with five minutes to spare.

I was at the start, but I didn't feel right. I had been nauseous all morning, but when the gun went off, so did I. My legs started feeling like they did in New Mexico. This place also had high altitude, and I had just completed 1,000 miles of driving. In addition, there was a spaghetti dinner (of course) the night before at Mount Rushmore. I knew this course had hills, one with a mile-and-a-half climb. I'd have to work. I decided to focus my mind on the scenery and try to ignore my body. It would not be ignored. My nausea and my leg tightness insisted on taking center stage. It sucked. Every lousy bit of it. The question, "Why am I doing this?' never went away. The back of my left leg was super tight. I knew if I took one long stride I would pull a hamstring. I could only shuffle the downhills, headed to the halfway point. This would be not only the run's halfway point, but my halfway through my 50 states and D.C. goal. I made the half and kept going, staring at the ground and calling myself an idiot.

On a steep downhill section I could feel my toes smashing into my shoes. Ouch! I tried to talk to a fellow runner, but she went on ahead of me. I don't remember anything of the scenery, just the pain. Despite all this, I crossed the finish in less than four hours and collapsed on the grass. Thank God it was over! At least it was another nonstopper. I tried my stomach with a small, small snack, a couple of grapes and a sip of water.

Time: 3:50:58

As soon as I showered we were ready to leave town. We headed east, and I barely made it three miles before the grapes returned. Then I felt better and was ready for a tourist stop in the Badlands, where we saw more prairie dogs and hundreds of buffalo. My stomach would be in better shape in Arkansas, where I would be able to taste some of the Southern fried foods.

28

Unexpected Fun
November 2, 2002

ARKANSAS   626 miles

Wynne was a weekend getaway for which we really didn't make a lot of plans. For a destination to qualify as being successful, it needs to have value for the entire family. Driving nine hours to Arkansas, running a marathon and driving nine hours back was not all that exciting. I was afraid this event would be a failure. Fortunately, about 45 miles west of Wynne is Memphis, and Jeanne has a cousin, Kathleen, who lives there. Visiting family always makes a trip worthwhile, so I signed up. Actually, we found a good attraction to be the restaurant we stopped at on our drive there. I was watching the clock, determined not to eat after 8 p.m. for an 8 a.m. run. Luckily, by seven, a billboard on the freeway announced, "Lambert's Restaurant: Home of the Throwed Rolls." The what? Well, it was food, so we stopped. The place was very large and packed with cars from all of the states.

Inside, we saw it was a place of nostalgia. The walls had business cards and photos sent from all over and an autographed photo of Jack Lambert, former linebacker for the Pittsburgh Steelers, as well as photos of the band Lynyrd Skynyrd. Between the decorated walls, there was a piano player. This was a happening place.

The food was happening, too. The waiters tossed bread rolls from across the dining room to us. We actually were able to catch them. The meal continued with gigantic mugs of drinks and plenty of bowls of all kinds of food. It was like being at grandmother's house in the 1940s—baked macaroni, tomatoes, baked potatoes, fried okra, meat loaf and molasses for the extra rolls that were arriving through the air. We were laughing like at a family meal, too. When we left, we had stuffed ourselves with Southern tastes, and the total bill was only $34. This place I would remember, and it formed a good beginning to our trip.

The Run

The thought of the meal made for a good start. My lack of sleep did not. Also, I'd had very little time to train. Well, I'd run under those conditions before, I could do it again. We took the van to the run, and I sat until the last minute, resting and staying warm. At the last minute I got out into the cool, crisp morning with a wind blowing around me. Jeanne got to watch. I told her that I probably wouldn't even break four hours this time.

She encouraged me, as always. "Just do your best and enjoy it."

"Most runners do enjoy this," I thought. Well, I did enjoy the marathons when I finally reached the finish line. I'd go for it.

The gun went off, and I was on my way. The first mile was against the wind: a slow 7:52. At least I didn't have the altitude problems of the last two runs. I took time to admire the back country, where we were running through trees, fields and rolling hills. Between miles seven and eight, I saw three very different types of snakes. Two were large, while the third was small and had black and white stripes.

I didn't take any fluids until I hit mile 15 because I had been feeling very nauseated, and if I had taken anything earlier, I would have thrown up. Around mile 17, I was passed by a man wearing a 50 States Club shirt. I sped up a little to keep his pace and conversed with him. It turned out this was Steve Boone, the founder of the 50 States Marathon Club. He was running in his 211th marathon. Our conversation inspired me to do two things after this run. The first was not to wait any longer to join the club. This was my 26th state, and I was way past being eligible. The second thing was to sign up for the Tulsa, Oklahoma run in November. It was a reunion run for 50–staters.

It wasn't long before Steve was moving just a little faster than I was. That was okay, because around the same time Jeanne and the kids drove by, stopped ahead of me, got out and cheered me on. They did this several times and really gave me a spark for running. But at the three–hour mark, mile 21, the course turned so that Jeanne couldn't follow any more. "I'll see you at the finish," she said. "I hope I make it there. I'm beginning to fall apart. I have lactate lock–up." She knew that meant my legs were getting tighter. I could have just quit and gotten in the warm van with her, but that wasn't my style, and she knew it.

She hesitated just a moment and then answered, "I'm sorry. I guess I'll see you there." It was only slightly in the tone of a question.

I answered what she expected. "See you," and she drove off.

I kept running. My miles became slower and slower. I knew it would be difficult to break four hours. At mile 22, I felt cold under the gloomy, overcast sky. It started to sprinkle. Mile 24 took me 12

minutes. When I approached
mile 26, I was at 3:57:48. I
still had two minutes and
twelve seconds to break the
four hours. As I came in view
of the waiting spectators, I
heard Jeanne scream, "Hurry,
Marlin, hurry." That little bit
of encouragement made all
the difference. I crossed the
line in just under four hours,
the last runner to do so. It
wasn't my best time by a long
shot, but I actually *enjoyed*
that finish. Maybe *because* it
was so close.

Time: 3:59:23

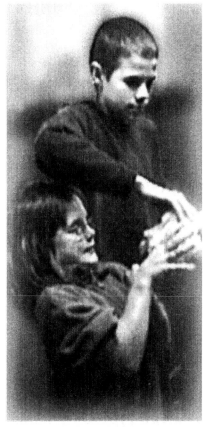

When we were all in the
van after the race, it was rain-
ing, but as we passed a cotton
field on the way to the hotel,
I stopped anyway. It was
good for the kids to get out
and run around picking a
few balls. A little further down I saw the cotton mill, and on a whim
I asked, "Does anyone want to see a cotton mill?"

"I do!" Austin's reply came quickly, so I made a U–turn and drove
in. In the office, I introduced myself and my family, and a man named
Roy gave us a complete tour of the working mill. Cool. We saw cotton dumped and then sucked up by a large vacuum. Then we saw the
seeds separated by a machine. (Imagine, people used to do that by hand).
At the end, the cotton went to another machine that tied it in bales. I
explained that cotton eventually became our clothes and sheets. I think
that places like this are the true value of these trips, better than all the artificial parks. This is life, and it was a big hit with us all.

Then it was back to the hotel for their kind of reality, the hotel
pool, while I soaked in a hot bath. That afternoon, we drove to

Memphis to meet Jeanne's cousin Kathleen at the world famous
Peabody Hotel. It is famous because it has ducks that live there.
Actually, ducks that live in quite high style. They have a penthouse
on the top of the hotel to stay in at night and a fountain pool in the
lobby to swim in during the day. The red carpet is rolled out for the
ducks to walk back to their penthouse on. Hundreds of people come
by every day to see the ducks parade by. When we arrived, they had
just left the pool and were walking their red carpet to the elevator. We
had a perfect view from the balcony above the fountain. That wasn't
the only view we had from that spot. I couldn't help myself. I had to
take a snapshot of the hostess directly below us, serving drinks in her
low cut shirt that revealed a great deal of cleavage. After watching the
hostess, I mean the ducks, we went with Kathleen and her boyfriend,
Rob, to the Spaghetti Warehouse and then back to the hotel. It was
good for Jeanne to relax with family, especially since her brother Ed
had passed away only four weeks before. It's always good for the kids
to stay connected with the larger family, to see they are part of a larg-

er whole. Erin sat on
Kathleen's lap and hugged
her. They looked more like
sisters than cousins once
removed. The run could have
been over four hours and it
still would have been worth
the trip for this moment. I
didn't like running that
much, but I liked what this
marathon quest was doing
for our family. Now I would
take Steve Boones advice,
and head for Tulsa.

29

Among The Elite
November 23, 2002

OKLAHOMA ✈ **697 miles**

The main obstacle for this trip was getting off the ground in the first place. We were standbys with hopes of flying to Tulsa by way of Houston. Jeanne brought the kids to the airport, where I had worked all day, and we went to the terminal. I was able to verify that the 757 had plenty of seats, so it should have been no problem. We passed security and waited. And waited. Then I heard a gate agent tell a lady, "Sorry, ma'am. There won't be anymore non–revs on this flight." Uh–oh. Time to head for the van. We had gathered our bags and were headed down the concourse when we heard, "Keesler, party of four. Keesler, party of four." Running to the podium, we were handed four passes. Then, as we started to the gate, she apologetically took the passes back. There were two people with the same seat (spinners). Luckily, that delay lasted just a few minutes, and we were back in line

111

with new passes. Soon, we were on the plane and up in the air. We weren't sitting together, but we would all arrive at the same time.

From my seat, I heard that a Continental executive was on board. I knew right away it was the then president (now CEO), Larry Kellner. He was sitting next to Jeanne. I passed her a note. "Be very good. You're sitting next to my boss. Could you get me an autograph? I could use it for my Tulsa story. M."

The flight attendant took the note and, in a few minutes, Larry himself came back and shook my hand. Cool. I was proud to be working for him. However, the stress wasn't quite over yet. All of the overhead bins were full and I was forced to check my bag. This flight had been delayed, which left very little time to make our connection to Tulsa once in Houston. On top of that, I had to run to the baggage carousel, retrieve my bag, then go back through security and run to what seemed like the farthest gate in the airport. Jeanne and the kids already had their seats and were wondering if I was even going to make it. I was out of breath and sweating, but I made it just in time. It was a relief when our plane landed in Oklahoma, where dozens of plaster penguins announced a new exhibit in their zoo. More than for penguins, Oklahoma is known for its oil wells, so the next morning, on the route to obtain our state sign photo, we stopped to check out some working wells. We watched some squeaky pumps bring up the oil.

We also visited another famous part of the state, the home of Will Rogers. It was well preserved with things used in the late 1800s, like lanterns, two wood stoves and a cistern for collecting rain as it rolled off the roof. Austin and Erin could see that children in Will's time never just turned on faucets like they do. It's good for all of us to remember how our ancestors lived to appreciate what we have. Since I worked on a farm myself, I had a better idea than they did. I was pleased at the informed, sensitive people they were becoming with our travels, despite what might be happening in classrooms. But whatever sights we saw or lessons they were absorbing, they always liked to end up playing in a pool. That's where I left them with Jeanne while I went to the 50 State Marathon Club meeting. During the awards ceremony, I felt like a little kid among a group of professional athletes. Not only was I among the sports elite, but I was conversing with them and getting their autographs. This group included

Norm Frank, who was only three marathons away from completing 800 runs! There was Ray Scharenbrock, who completed the 50 states seven times; and Rick Worley, who is a record holder for running 200 marathons in 159 consecutive weekends. I saw Bob Lehew, the club president, and Steve and Paula Boone, who have achieved celebrity status in Houston contributing to marathons. Also, Steve has run over 200 marathons and Paula was approaching 100. There were others who were receiving their trophies for having run the 50 states. That was a trophy I now felt I had a chance to receive someday. After the awards, I went to meet Jeanne and the kids and brought them back to the Hilton for the pre–race pasta dinner. I told Jeanne about all the people I'd met.

"You're doing great, yourself, Marlin. You're my hero," she said. I didn't need any medals.

While we dined on gourmet pasta, we were entertained with speeches. We learned that this marathon was a fund raiser for Cal Farley's Boys Ranch, and the Tulsa Boys' Home. Several members of the Boys Ranch were marathon participants. One of the boys gave a testimonial speech on how the ranch had turned his troubled life around. Then we were treated to the words of Dr. Brent Weigner. He not only had completed the 50 states, but he was the first to complete an ultramarathon, one in each continent. This included runs in the Sahara Desert and Antarctica. Despite all this, his greatest accomplishment was surviving cancer twice. When he acknowledged his introduction, he commented, "Of all the introductions I've ever had, yours (pause) was the most recent." Hearty laughs from all of us. I hoped to add his signature to my collection of autographs. First, I had to add another run to my goal.

The Run

The marathon, on Saturday morning, was along the Arkansas River under clear, cool skies. Jeanne went along to watch the start. I did a little warmup on a path by the car and almost ran into a fox. I was inspired and felt that this was where I belonged. Close to the start, we were all given balloons, which we released before the gun went off. It was a beautiful beginning. I was off with a decent pace, more relaxed than I had been in any run before this. Maybe I was really becoming a part of the sport. The course was not only by the river, but through a park, out and back, so I saw everything twice. The second time through I saw Jeanne and the kids cheering me on and taking photos. That certainly helped, although my pace did slow down progressively after mile 14. Then, at mile 24, when I was really sore, a man rode by on a bike with Gatorade. Boy, did I need that. When I crossed the finish line, I knew then why I was doing marathons. It just feels so good to reach the finish and stop. The more I think about it, the more I like that word, "*stop.*" I think I have a special bond with it. Even better than stopping is seeing my cheering family wait.

Time: 3:37:46

To make this trip even better, we were invited to Bob Lehew's house for an after–run party. We all watched the Ohio State–Michigan game, and Ohio State won. Yahoo! Austin had a blast playing with the neighbor's dog, and Erin, playing with a baby. I added more names to my autograph collection, that of Gary Julin, a 55–year–old runner who had completed 106 marathons in under three hours, and that of Dr. Weigner. As the doctor put his pen to my paper, I looked at him with awe and told him, "Of all the autographs I've obtained, yours (pause) is the most recent." He responded with, "I wonder where you got that from?" We both chuckled. This was now the cream of all the marathons to that date, and I had been in some really great ones. By the end of the party, it was early afternoon and time to celebrate Austin's birthday. We drove around, stopping wherever Austin wanted to stop. One such place was the Oral Roberts University campus. The second was the Texas Roadhouse for dinner. While we waited for dessert, the waitress brought out a wooden horse with a saddle. She had Austin sit on it while she announced, "It's Austin Keesler's birthday!" Everyone in the restaurant gave him a loud, "Yahoo!" It was entertaining to watch his big grin. It was a great place to celebrate. On the flight home, Jeanne agreed that number 28 was a wonderful time. She also hinted in advance of February that marathon number 30, almost on our anniversary, would be a romantic time to receive a replacement diamond ring. I still didn't have the money for the kind of ring I wanted to give her, so I just took her hand and softly told her to quit pestering me about it.

30

A Run For Fuzzhead
January 18, 2003

NORTH CAROLINA 816 miles

North Carolina was more of a relaxed getaway, not a memorable vacation. On the flight down, we were somehow pegged for high security check, after all our travels, I guess. When they found I was an O'Hare employee, I didn't have to remove my shoes and open my bags. Jeanne and the kids were not so lucky. We finally boarded, and they slept. We arrived in Charlotte along with a snowstorm that practically paralyzed the state. The city was clean, with a beautiful skyline, but all wrapped in white. Even the downtown waterfall was frozen. In this weather, we couldn't make it to the Smokey Mountains as planned, so we just drove around in the scenic hills with no destination in mind. It was calm and peaceful with few people on the road. Then, of course, Austin and Erin wanted their pool time, this time indoors in the hotel. Warm and dry, we all went to a restaurant that was part of a brewery, taking a tour of the place. That was the extent of our sightseeing for this state. It was time to rest for the run.

This run was dedicated to our dog, Fuzzhead, who had just gone up to doggy heaven right after Christmas. Fuzz had been with us for over 14 years. She was a part of the family. There are a dozen tales to show how dear she was, but my favorite was of her on the beach with Austin back in Hawaii. Austin was almost 2, and I took him and Fuzz to the beach while Jeanne worked one evening. Sand crabs were scrambling everywhere. Fuzzhead went nuts. She chased one, and it buried itself in the sand, so she started digging, snorting and sniffling the whole time. As he watched her dig, Austin began to giggle. His laughter was so genuine, it made me laugh. Fuzz had a hole about two feet deep when she raised her head, shaking it furiously. A large crab had latched itself to her nose. She shook her head until the crab went flying across the sand. Then she kept on shaking her head as if the crab was still there. It turned out that one claw stayed attached to her nose, and as I reached to pull it off, Austin giggled even more. Thank you, Fuzz, for that memory and laughter. Animals can often reach children with special needs better than a human. Fuzz was our treasure.

That's why it was so tough when she passed on. She had been ill for a while. At 14, she was like a human of 98, they say, and she was in pain. Her back legs were giving out, so that she could barely stand. I knew that the best thing for her was to have her put out of her suffering, but I couldn't bear to do it. I waited so she could have Christmas with us, but on Christmas Day she was worse, losing all her strength in her back legs. On the morning of the 27th, when the kids were asleep and Jeanne was at work, I knew what I had to do. The one–mile drive to the vet was the longest mile I'd ever driven. She lay in the seat next to me trembling, as if she knew what was going to happen. I had called ahead, so I just walked solemnly into the vet's office and laid her on the table, watching her shake, and waited. The vet injected a solution into her vein, and in a second the shaking stopped. She was gone. The vet asked if there were anything else she could do for me. My chin was trembling and I couldn't talk, so I just shook my head no. Immediately I went to the van, where tears streamed down my cheeks. This was the first time I had really cried since I was 16, when my boss, who had me working in his strawberry fields, had been killed by a drunk driver. This hit me hard. It was even tougher later that morning, when Austin and Erin had just finished their bowls of cereal and put them on the floor for Fuzz to lap up the little extra milk. I told them we could no longer do that. A few minutes later, I was standing on the stairwell listening to Erin consoling Austin. She complained, "Austin, we have the meanest dad ever." Fuzz had been our friend. When I worked nights and slept days, she always laid in bed right next to me. She always laid her head on my lap when we watched TV. She was a joyful member of our family, and this run was for her.

The Run

Saturday morning was clear, but only 19 degrees. There was ice on my moustache. Fortunately, the runners had a warm place to hang out before the run. When I went down to the run, there were reporters and cameras all over. I stayed away, as I'm not fond of being interviewed, but I was glad this was well publicized. I concentrated on my warmup sprints, but they were not warming me up. It was just too cold. This was the first marathon where I wore polypropylene thermal underwear. As soon as the run started, I knew this was going to be a rough one for me. The course was fine, but, as usual, I had not trained enough. The speed was just not there. I remember looking up at times and observing the budding trees and thinking this would be a lovely place in the spring, but mostly I just had my head down, putting one foot in front of the other. It was a very nice, flat course, and I was able to see Charlotte's superb skyline from miles away. At last, the cold miles were over, barely under four hours, but under, and my team was waiting. After I rested a minute, Jeanne told me that one of the runners had collapsed on the 26th mile and had been rushed to the hospital. The next day I checked on the internet and found out he was fine, but I thought they should have carried his stretcher the rest of the way over the finish before they put him in the ambulance. I guess that's how runners think. I could certainly say I was one now, ready for Alabama. I had a month to prepare, if time actually allowed it. Nice cold run. Fuzz, we will miss you.

Time: 3:57:58

31

In Good Company
February 9, 2002

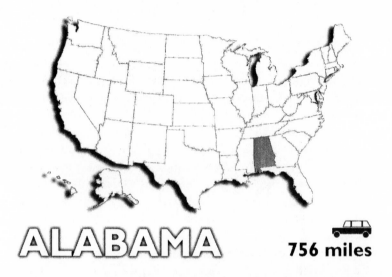

ALABAMA

🚙 **756 miles**

For Alabama, we planned well, so the state was a winner. However, before I begin with all of the good stuff, I must acknowledge a couple of things I did prior to our departure that would qualify me as an idiot. Note I gave myself that name. You don't need to add to it, although you may want to when you read what I did. First of all, I am supposed to wear steel–toe shoes at work. I'm in cargo, remember? For the previous six months, though, I had been sneaking my feet into comfortable running shoes because the steel–toe jobs had been bothering my knees. Mistake. I was recounting and restacking a 500–piece shipment of boxes onto wooden skids. I took one box off and walked to another skid to restack it, but as I did this I rammed my right foot right into the corner of the protruding skid. "Ouch!" and a few other words with four letters. I dropped

the box and hobbled around
screaming. Somehow I kept
working, mumbling various
expletives, and it wasn't until I
got home to take off my shoe
and sock that I saw the damage:
blood and a ripped–off toenail.
Not the best way to prepare for a

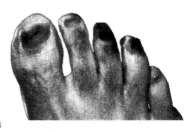

run. That same day, my brain must have been in the wrong gear
because I made another clever move. The gas bill arrived, and it
was triple the amount of the month before. We had to conserve,
and what better time than when we were going to be out of town.
Wednesday, just before we left, I turned the thermostat down to
54 degrees. It was going to get cold, and I didn't want to pay to
heat a house we weren't going to be in anyway. So, dear reader,
thou mayest wonder a bit longer what the connection was
between turning down the heat and being an idiot. So, with my
toe properly bandaged and our home nice and cool, we took off
early to beat the traffic. Before we headed to Alabama, we stopped
first in southern Kentucky to visit a dear friend, Betty Park.
Having come from a broken home, of sorts, when I was 16, I had
stayed in Father Patrick O'Donnel's rectory. Father Pat was a Telly
Savalas lookalike. He was completely bald, had a deep booming
voice, and he was very committed to his calling. He once told me
that, "The more you know the more responsibility you will have."

Betty and Mary Elliot, another great friend, helped take care of
me during my junior year of high school. They helped make this a
great time in my life. And later, Father Pat performed our wedding
ceremony and baptized Austin. This visit included introducing the
kids to Betty, as well as to her granddaughter, Elizabeth, and
great–granddaughter, Emily. It was a good homecoming, with stories
of the teenage me and what was happening now to all of us. One of
my favorite stories was about doing the laundry at Father Pat's. From
the age of 11, I had always bought my own clothes with money I
earned. One day, I filled the washing machine up with my brand new
school clothes, which included my treasured REO Speedwagon concert shirt. It was my first major concert, and wearing that shirt to
school was very important to me, so I was going to make sure I got

all of my laundry extra clean. I stuffed the washing machine full, putting the REO Speedwagon Tour 1982 shirt on top. I put the laundry soap in and then reached up on the shelf in front of me and grabbed the jug of bleach and poured it on top. As the bleach landed on my clothes, the colors changed right before my eyes. My clothes were ruined forever, and I had just received my first big lesson in being a bachelor.

From Kentucky, we went down to Tennessee and toured the Saturn automobile factory. Factories seem to be fun for the kids, watching how things are made. This was an especially happy place because the employees were always smiling and waving at us as they worked. I asked about this and learned they work in task oriented groups, with no supervisors and no time clocks. A good idea that makes for what I consider good, safe products. They test them all with crash dummies, and Erin had a chance to pose with one. From future cars, it was back to the past, in a visit to the Meriwether Lewis monument. This is where Lewis, of Lewis and Clark fame, committed suicide on his way back to Washington, D.C. He was buried in that pioneer cemetery. Standing there, I thought in reverence of all the people who have helped to make this land what it is today, and I silently thanked them.

After that, we braved snow, rain, and darkness to reach Huntsville. This town is famous for its space center. Here we were real pilots, landing a space shuttle (on a simulator, of course). We also went on a centrifuge ride and a virtual Mars roller coaster ride. This was topped off with a panoramic IMAX movie in a planetarium—style dome. We felt like we were really exploring space from an international space station. Then it was back down to earth and on to Birmingham. Time to remember I was there to run. I picked up my runner's packet and took the kids for a hotel swimming marathon of their own. By the next morning we were all rested enough for another visit. This time it was to Jeanne's relatives in Montgomery, a town of hanging Spanish moss. There, Uncle Bob and Aunt Mary Anne gave us a warm family welcome. Bob is on oxygen because of his heart and lungs, and he had lost a leg to diabetes, but he still manages to be in good spirits. They both wished me well on my next day's run. This visit was even more meaningful, especially to Jeanne, because Uncle Bob passed away later on that year.

The Run

Despite the well wishes, I was at the start two hours early because
I couldn't sleep. There was a light breeze, and it was freezing cold. I
didn't really want to run, but I knew I'd warm up once I started, so I
welcomed the gun at 7:03. I felt quicker than three weeks before in
Charlotte, and this course had rows of well–wishers cheering us on
and bands playing. I started to get in the groove. There was a hill at
mile 9 that put me behind time, but a band played the Rocky theme
song and kept us moving. At the top, the view of Birmingham was
gorgeous and a bagpipe player was waiting to serenade us.

Then, out of nowhere, I saw a sign that read, "Way to Go,
Marlin." It was being held by Shaheen, daughter of Carla , the
administrative specialist where I work, and her boyfriend, Michael.
They live in Birmingham and came out to give me a little extra boost.
I needed that. I was doing all right. Suddenly, smash! That was my
foot hitting a protruding piece of concrete on a bridge overpass.
That's all I needed. I took a momentous–type spill, throwing my
body into contortions. I twisted my left knee. If this had been a training run, I would have quit. As it was, I just decelerated and kept
going somehow. Then I came down with a case of the
"squeezed–cheek syndrome," but I just held them tightly together
and moved right by the porta–potty that was calling my name. At the
very end, I poured on my last bit of energy and was able to pass the
man in front of me for a finish just under four hours. There were
Michael and Shaheen and, right behind them, Jeanne and the kids. I
was glad I had boosted myself on, even with the fall. I do enjoy reaching the finish and stopping. I had even forgotten my sore toe.

Time: 3:57:57

Driving back through a heavy treacherous snowstorm, we
stopped again at Betty's. She welcomed us with warm plates of
spaghetti. She also watched the kids while Jeanne and I visited other
friends. We stopped to see Lester Lannom, who had sold me my
motorcycle when I was 15 and taught as a substitute teacher in my
junior high. He was 93 on this visit, but he remembered that I drove
that motorcycle all the way from Cleveland to Palm Springs,
California. I couldn't forget that trip either. It's when I started being
myself, Marlin. I had to get on my old motorcycle and get out of

Ohio. I had just finished high school, and I was being evicted from what had been home for the past six months. The father found out I had a relationship with his daughter, my high school friend. "I want you out *this week!*"

I decided to try my luck staying with my sister in southern California. Our father had died a violent death, our stepfather an early one, and our mother had gone away with a loser. My sister offered me a place while I looked for work. That was a start.

To leave, I borrowed money from the Catholic Church and shipped my belongings. Now I needed to get my paycheck without telling my boss, Joe, that I was leaving. He was the one who had shared my confidence with the family I was staying with, so I was ready to leave him. We had a big assignment to cut wood and build pallets. We cut in the morning and built in the afternoon. I asked for my pay at lunch so I could run to the bank. He paid me and I never went back. By 12:30 I was on I–90 heading west, with a full gas tank and a full belly. It wasn't really enough for the trip across the country to Palm Springs. I battled strong winds in Oklahoma, had a flat tire in Amarillo, Texas, and had to use most of my money to have it fixed. I ended up pleading for gas money, getting police vouchers for gas and ultimately receiving a wire for $50 in Flagstaff, Arizona from my sister's boyfriend. I finally made it to her house, exhausted and hungry. Despite the trip, I had really enjoyed the scenery along the way. I promised myself I'd come back with time and money, and most of all, with someone to share it with and see all of the United States. I never dreamed it would be with marathons. California wasn't what I expected. I had found a job quickly, but, just as quickly, rent and food took it all. This wasn't going to work. I went right down to the Air Force recruiter and signed up. Now, in a way, I had family, but not the kind I wanted. This kind fed and clothed me and told me what to do, but there was nothing personal. That would come soon afterward.

Now, visiting Lester, I smiled over at the loves I had today, Jeanne, Austin, and Erin. I could not erase the pains of the past, but with them I was forming a future. Next was Ed and Dorothy Slack's home. Ed was a banker and farmer who once lent me 10 dollars to see a three–ring circus, and later gave me a job in the tobacco and soybean fields. His house was where I had lived when I was 15, so I told Jeanne more about those days. It was a nice place to be, so close to our anniversary. Again, I wished I had the money to slip a new diamond on her hand. Later we went back to pick up the kids and resume our long drive back home. We returned to a freezing cold home with frozen pet fish. Some *idiot* had turned off the heat and they all died. Before Kansas, I'd have a talk with that idiot.

32

In The News
March 29, 2003

KANSAS

670 miles

In Kansas, I had the honor of being in the newspaper. Naturally, I glowed and bought ten extra copies. This came about because the race director, June DeWeese, and I exchanged quite a few emails before I went. This was the inaugural run in Abilene, and to promote it, June wrote up some runners' profiles and sent them to the local newspaper. Knowing in advance that I was going to be in the paper, I felt an incentive for extra training in the coming six weeks. Secretly, I was going to shoot for a Boston qualification. This meant a 3:15 finish. The first weekend after the Birmingham run, I put in 40 miles in three days. Good, except my left knee became sore and a little swollen. I rested a few days, and then I put in another 31 miles over a three–day period the following weekend. My friend Layne was covering 60 miles a week. That was my goal, to do 60 miles a week, too, for at least two weeks before that marathon. Well, for various reasons, including soreness, snow and a fear of injury, my mileage just plummeted. Mentally, I went back to the state of mind where I needed to make sure I did just enough to break four hours. It's a sad thing to relegate one's mind to mediocrity, which is what I had done.

Well, at least we could have some fun there, whatever time I turned out to have. We had planned this trip for months. Austin and Erin would be on spring break, and we had relatives to stay with in the state. Our first stop in Kansas was in the small town of Eskridge, to visit my Aunt Mary and Uncle Don. When you look up the word "fun" in the dictionary, it says, "Synonym for Aunt Mary." She is a blast to be around. Of course, her capacity to count beyond 10 is somewhat limited. She told me the population of Eskridge was 500 people, about the same population it had over 100 years ago. She was wrong. I walked around this little town and only counted 72.

This visit was only the second time I had met my aunt. The first time was at the memorial service for my mother after her death in April of 2000. So, during this trip, we really took some time to get to know each other while the kids took their time to get to know her many cats and kittens.

We became very fond of a special kitten, Gizmo, who thought it was her job to make sure Jeanne and I had as little sleep as possible. If I moved my foot, the kitten would attack it. Gizmo would purr and sniff our ears, and then crawl under the blanket. This tiny friend was a welcome addition to the population of the town. However, we also wanted to see towns with a few more people and sights.

During our first day in Kansas, we drove over to Kansas City, Missouri, and visited the Steamboat Arabia Museum. This boat hit a snag in the Missouri River in 1856 and sank. The river changed course, and the boat was forgotten. Then, in 1988, it was uncovered in a farmer's field. The treasures from this steamboat are on display at the museum. Kansas is a state full of history. It's in the minds of the people, passed down from grandparents, and in a great number of museums. After seeing the one for the steamboat, we went the next day to see the Museum of History in Topeka. There, under the roof, is a full–sized Cheyenne tipi and a covered wagon, stocked and ready for travel, and, from more recent times, a 1950s diner. In between museums, you can see the grooves of a pioneer wagon wheel or wild berries growing. The state is a mixture of little towns, cities and quiet, isolated prairies. After Topeka, we went south to Wichita, the largest city in Kansas, where we visited my cousin Shannon. As with Aunt Mary, my first meeting with Shannon had been at a funeral, that of my father's mother. I saw her again at the funeral of my father's father. With such distance between families, it often happens that way. I was glad to be meeting her at a much happier time. She had promised by email to receive us with a homemade apple pie, and she kept her word. It was delicious. Later on we went with Shannon and her kids to the Wichita Greyhound Park and watched the dog races. Wow! I envied their speed. Of course, they have four legs. While there, we bet $50, taking turns picking the winners. We left the park with 19 dollars and having enjoyed the afternoon. This was something neat that the kids were really into. The next day it was time to head to the marathon city, Abilene. This town was ready for a marathon. There were "Welcome Marathoner" signs everywhere. We had lunch at the famous Kirby House restaurant, where the entire staff wore marathon shirts. I liked this town from the moment we drove in. After lunch, we checked out the famous Abilene boyhood home of President Eisenhower and the Eisenhower Museum. In those, we saw exhibits from his childhood and his days as a leader in World War II, as well as memorabilia of the White House.

Nearby, we paid our respects at the place of meditation where he, his wife and firstborn son's remains are. I had just read his biography, so his home made the book come alive. I tried to impress on the kids how important this man was to our country. I pulled a dime out of my pocket to show them his likeness on it. I always took advantage of any opportunities to remind them of Dwight Eisenhower, like when we passed the occasional sign that read, "Eisenhower Interstate System." Also, in a day I would be running a marathon in his honor. After the Eisenhower Center, we walked across the street and spent time in the Greyhound Hall of Fame. Having seen the dogs run, we had a fondness for them. There we learned a great deal about the history of the greyhounds, greyhound racing and greyhound adoptions. The information on adoptions really tweaked our interest, since we had just been through the passing of Fuzzhead. The cashier informed us that usually it's the older dogs that are up for adoption after their racing days, but at this time there were also some puppies in need of

a home. They were in a house down the
street, the one with junk on the porch.
We said we'd probably check it out, but
now we had to go tour the marathon
course. It was an out–and–back type of
course with only minor hills. As we
drove back, we passed a couple of greyhound farms along the way. We
stopped at one where a dog was giving
birth. There were pups of all ages, and
we were allowed to pet them. The dogs
on this farm were so friendly and affec-
tionate that the kids just wanted to stay
and play with them. The idea of having
a greyhound was growing stronger. The
owner showed us one of his tools, a
whirligig, used for training the dogs. He

explained their diets and training. They certainly seemed well taken
care of. Still inspired, we went back to town and found the house with
junk on the porch. The owner invited us in, and I saw there was only
a small path between his stacks of boxes and stuff on either side. At the
other end of the room his wife's head could barely be seen sticking out
above the stuff. The owner said it would be better if we just went on
out back to see the puppies. He said we could take one or all of them
for that matter. We worked our way through a wooden fence and
around collections of I–don't–know–what to find happy, playful pups.
We played with the puppies and would have taken one or two home
with us if home were not three days and 1,000 miles away. However,
this confirmed that we were ready to bring another dog into our home.
For now, I had a race to run. I'd been having so much fun being a
tourist and a guest; I had to get myself ready to actually run.

On Friday morning, I picked up my packet and had the pleasure
of meeting June, the race director, for the first time in person. I could
feel the anxiety exuding from her and her staff as they continued to
work hard at making this a successful event. I really wanted to do well
in this run, but I hadn't trained enough. I had to tell myself, "Just
move on with life, Marlin." I couldn't dwell on it. Everything else was
going well. We were still seeing many sights and people. We went to

see Abilene's Heritage Center, where colorful quilts of all designs were on display, and then we experienced the evolution of the telephone in the Museum of Telegraphy. Such a long way since the first greetings were called out from one room to another to today's cell phones that can carry your voice anywhere. "We've learned to communicate faster, but do we communicate any better?" I wondered.

In keeping with our trip to the past, we rode a 102–year–old carousel. For a moment, rising up and down on a painted horse to the lively circus music, I didn't think about the marathon.

After the carousel we toured an area called Abilene Town that basically was a western setting of old 1800s town buildings. This place gave us a deeper appreciation of just what Abilene was to this country. It is considered the first real cow town. This came about when the railroad laid down tracks through Abilene. The cattle ranchers made their cattle drives from all over the West to Abilene, where the cows could be put on trains and shipped out. This immersion into the real western history made me proud to walk around with my marathon shirt on that read, "I ran the Chisholm trail."

We came back to the present later Friday afternoon when we hooked up with my friend, Layne, and his wife, CJ, and had dinner at Mr. K.'s Farmhouse Restaurant. This was quality time in a classy place. I was more relaxed about the marathon by then.

The Run

The night before the run, Shannon and her two daughters, Kaylynne and Greta, came to the hotel so they could join Jeanne and the kids in my cheering squad. Aunt Mary and Uncle Don arrived, too. In addition, my friend Layne, who was also running, and his wife C.J. were there. The next morning we met up with June and her staff, who were brimming with excitement. Add to that the fact that the paper wrote about me. With all those well–wishers and the publicity, this was one run where I really wanted to be in top form and set a PR. I knew, however, that it probably wasn't going to happen. I should just move on with life and enjoy the marathon itself and all the people.

When I started the run it was 29 degrees, with a wind blowing 25 miles an hour. Fortunately, it was blowing from behind, so I shed my sweats and let myself be carried forward, feeling a false sense of swiftness. The neatest thing that happened during the run was near the 3–mile mark, where some volunteers, placed to make sure runners didn't follow the wrong path, were listening to a play by play of the run on their car radio. As I came within listening distance, I distinctly heard: "…Now let me tell you about another runner, Marlin Keesler, who is…" At that point I had passed their car and was out of hearing range. Oh, boy. What I would have given to have heard the rest. I wanted to stop and say, "Hey, that's me he's talking about."

I sped on, motivated by the bit I heard. A little further on I passed the greyhound farm we had visited. The owner and his family were out cheering the runners on. He informed me that I was the 40th runner to pass by. Not bad, since over half of them were only running a half–marathon. Further on I saw Jeanne, Shannon and the kids. "Way to go, Marlin." "Keep it up, Dad."

This run had more of my private supporters than any so far, and I was energized. I zipped along, averaging 7:30 per mile. Then I made a turn and slammed into a strong cross wind. All the glory of a great time ended at that point. It felt as if a giant hand were pushing against me. I felt like the Bob Seger song, "Against the Wind." I sang that song in my mind for the next few miles until the tune changed to a Jim Croce song, "You Don't Mess Around with Jim." There's a line in the song that says that you don't spit in the wind. Well, I did. What a mess!

By the turnaround point, I thought I'd at least have a decline to help me, but no. It was an incline. I remembered my grandparents saying they walked to school uphill both ways. That's how I felt I was going. Worse, my friend Layne, who was 51, passed me. That wasn't supposed to happen, and I was reaching my lactate threshold. I'd just have to keep going and not think of time.

There, at last, in front of me was the finish, and I trotted over and relaxed, feeling good that it at least had been a nonstopper. Everyone was congratulating me on completing another run, and I received my medal, grinning. Maybe for the next one, in Wyoming, I'd be faster. Now I was just glad to be with people who loved me and finally *not* running.

Time: 3:54:59

After the marathon, we went back to Wichita, this time with Shannon, Aunt Mary and Uncle Don. Along the way we stopped at an old fort on Coronado Heights with an imaginary view of old Indian wars and a present day one of the land for miles around. Once back in Wichita, we went to the Prairie Rose Chuck Wagon. Hawaii has it luaus and Kansas has its equivalent, the Chuck Wagon. We drove several miles out of town to a working ranch. Prior to our western–style meal, we were treated to a hay ride, with the wagon pulled by horses. Then we sat down and enjoyed huge helpings of brisket, baked beans and everything else that's part of a trail ride meal. While we were eating, we were entertained by the Prairie Rose Wranglers, a western band made up of the same guys who served our meal. Their versatility had no boundaries. These guys were great singers and performed a class A show. Aunt Mary bought us one of their CDs, and we have played it on every trip since. After eating and right before the music began, all of the little kids were taken away by a cowboy. When the show was over, they all came back and went up on stage with an encore of "Deep In the Heart of Texas." Erin had a blast singing on stage with the other kids. I wished school could be like that for her.

From there we went on to Kansas City, so Jeanne could see her cousin Stephanie. We shared a catch–up on news over breakfast at the Machine Shack Restaurant. Relatives beat the sights any time, and we were sorry to leave the state. On the drive home we shared stories of our favorite parts of the trip. One part we agreed on was how much we liked the greyhounds. Jeanne and I decided we would look into adopting one. First, I had to rest for my next run.

33

Outlaw Cave
June 1, 2003

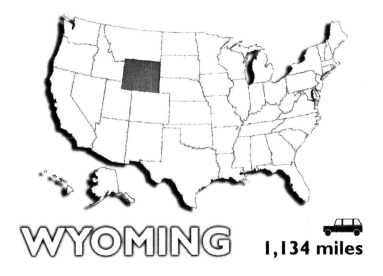

WYOMING 1,134 miles

This marathon was one of three in 14 days. Rushed, but worth it. The kids were on summer vacation, and Jeanne and I had two weeks of vacation together for the first time in our 15 years of marriage. We were glad to be going, even though it was an 18–hour drive from Chicago to Casper, Wyoming. Before the drive, I had worked until 12:45 a.m. and picked up the crew a half-hour later. So by the time we arrived and I picked up my runner's packet, I had been awake for 40 hours. Still, I tossed and turned, worrying that I might oversleep and miss the run.

The Run

The best part was that the marathon was before the fun. It began on a cool, absolutely gorgeous morning, and left from the Casper Events Center on the top of a hill. The scenery at this elevation, almost a mile high, was awesome. At this point I didn't care that I only had two 14–mile training runs and two nine–mile runs under my belt in preparation for this race. I didn't mind that I had just driven 1,000 miles, with only four hours of sleep in two days. It was just one of those perfect moments, and I was savoring every bit of it. I think, for the first time, I didn't feel nervous about a marathon.

At 6:30 the run began. The first mile was flat and seemed to go okay. Because of the elevation, I expected my legs to be tight, but they weren't. My only problem was catching my breath. All of my first four miles were under eight minutes each. Then, after the fourth mile, there was a hill that really challenged my breathing. I tried to talk to another runner next to me, but finally had to say, "Good Luck. I can't keep up with you. Go ahead." I needed my breath for running.

The theme of the marathon was "Run With the Pronghorn." Boy, did we ever.

The pronghorns, a type of antelope, were running in herds all around us. They ran in the fields and back and forth across our path.

Not only did I see pronghorns, but spectacular views. I could see a rainstorm over Casper, with lightning and dark clouds, but we remained dry. Then we ran through parks and along the Platte River. I thought to myself, which was rare for a marathon, "There's nothing I'd rather be doing (except maybe walking)."

Around mile 10, I was lucky enough to run beside marathon legend Brent Weigner. However, not for long. He moved on ahead as I was slowing my pace. Not long after that I started to hurt. Remember that I said earlier I didn't care that I hadn't done much training? At this point, I cared. By mile 20, I was losing my appreciation for the beauty around me. I still had a chance to be under four hours, but my minutes per mile were increasing. By mile 24, I tried to keep moving by saying to myself, "I care. I care." Still, mile 24 took nearly 11 minutes. I knew I would have to do some rocking and rolling to get the 1.2 miles left in under 10 minutes. I sped up, then slowed down with the pain, and then sped up again. I don't know how I did it, but despite the pain and the altitude, I still made it in less than four hours.

Time: 3:59:18

Now it was time to play. Reading about the area, we chose to visit Outlaw Cave, supposedly the place where Butch Cassidy and the Sundance Kid once hid out. Had I known how hidden it was, we might have forgotten the idea, but I didn't, so we blissfully set out. It was literally at the end of nowhere, if ever a place was. Twenty miles from the freeway, we went from paved to gravel road. Eight miles later, we went from gravel to a road washed out, rutted with large stones, a one–lane road made for four–wheelers. It took 45 minutes to go 10 miles. At the end, we were in a campground high up next to the cliffs along the Platte River in the middle of the Big Horn Mountains. No more road. There was a small sign with an arrow pointing down a path. They must be kidding. After a minute's debate, I decided, "Why not? Let's go." We worked our way down a treacherous path and heard a scream. Austin and Erin had found a long black and yellow snake. By the time Jeanne and I got there, it was slithering away. Moving on. In 45 minutes we were at the bottom. The view was worth the difficult walk. But that wasn't all. Then we had to follow an even

smaller path along the river. That's where we walked on areas 50 feet up with nothing to grasp as we shuffled our way around a ledge. The kids seemed to enjoy the danger. I had doubts. If we didn't find that cave soon, we were going back. Just then we saw a cave 15 feet deep and 7 feet tall. I didn't know for sure if it was Outlaw Cave, but for me, it certainly was. We talked about the outlaws and their visit here, posed for photos, and then I was glad to head back to the camping area.

Once up there, it became very dark, and we put up the tent as quickly as we could. It was up just in time, as it began to pour. Then, within 15 minutes, the sun was shining, and we saw a double rainbow of biblical proportions. It stayed light until 10, so we roasted hot dogs and marshmallows. It doesn't get any better than that. After what seemed like a short rest, we witnessed a grand sunrise. We packed and headed for a visit to Montana (see Montana).

P.S. Six days later, after leaving Montana, we were back in Wyoming, where we decided to revisit Devil's Tower, the mountain with the straight up and down sides. Last time, we had just looked. This time, since we had an extra day to play with, we were hoping to go horseback riding and camping in the campground next to it. We stopped at the stables that advertised horseback riding only to find out the trail rides had not yet begun. If we were going to camp out at Devil's Tower, we needed to find something to do. So we figured we would dwell on it over breakfast at a nearby place called the Family Restaurant. While sitting in our booth, we couldn't help noticing numerous enlarged photographs of some people climbing the tower. One photo was of an older, heavy-set guy, and another was of a couple of kids not older than 14. The pictures were very intriguing. I asked the waiter about them, and it turned out he was the guy in the picture. I instantly thought, "If this guy can do it, so can I." At this point I noticed my heart rate had increased just a little. When the waiter brought our meals, I inquired about the climb. He said it took him four hours to climb it. He also stated that there were guides, albeit pricey, who worked with novices all the way up. This was an adventure I did not want to pass up, even though my racing heart was trying to tell me something different. In my mind, I blocked every reality out except the one of seeing myself on top. Who cared if I was terrified of heights? If that old man and those two kids could do it, so could I. After breakfast we drove to the guide shack. Walking into this place, my heart was beating so fast I could hardly talk. The man there, who looked like a climber, was very informative. He explained details of the climb and the various cost structures of having a guide and renting the equipment. I figured I could actually afford this. Oh, man, my heart was doing some pumping now. Then, with one simple question and quick response, he gave me the most cathartic feeling of relief I have ever felt in my entire life. He asked if I had ever done any rock climbing. I said, "No". He replied that rule such and such required a minimum of two days training before attempting to climb the tower. Well, we didn't have two days to hang around there. Whew! How bummed out I wasn't to hear that.

With no horseback riding and no climbing the tower, we really did not have a good reason to stay. So we just spent a couple of hours walking the trails around the base, looking up at other climbers. I was thinking, "They've got to be nuts." Then we continued on our long

drive east. We favored going back for another look at Mount Rushmore and the Crazy Horse Memorial. We were lucky on the second one. At a rest stop, Jeanne overheard that this was the one day a year that people were allowed to climb to the top of the memorial. It was the day of the annual Volksmarch, a 10K walk to the top of

Crazy Horse. There was only one small problem, registration would close at 1p.m., and it was already 12:25, and we were 56 miles away. Not possible, but I was going to try anyway. We jumped in the van and I drove as quickly as possible. Despite my efforts, we were at the tent area 25 minutes late. People were parking in fields far away and walking, but I drove right up in front of the tents and ... bingo! A spot opened up. Maybe we were destined to make the walk, but we still had to be registered. Hopeful walkers were being turned away. I approached the man who seemed to be directing things. He was about to turn us away when I showed him my 50 States book. "This could help increase exposure for the memorial," I pleaded. He glanced at the book and seemed to agree. "Okay. You want to go to the top?" "You bet!" He handed me his last four registration cards to complete, and we went to join the other walkers. Actually, at our pace, we were soon passing others. Even Erin was able to keep up. In an hour and 40 minutes, we were standing at the top by the gigantic head. The view was awesome, walking around the gigantic head of the famous Native American. It's an experience that can't be beat. I had said when I first saw the memorial that I would come back in 20 years, and here I was less than a year later. When we came down we visited the museum to learn more about Crazy Horse. It was just a perfect ending for this part of our trip, and just think, earlier that morning we were planning on staying at Devil's Tower for the whole day. We *will* be back.

34

Austin Is King of the Mountain
June 7, 2003

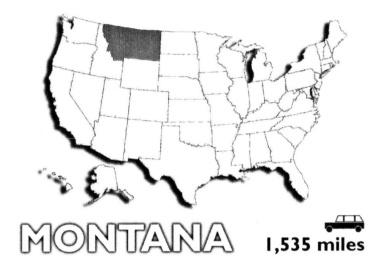

MONTANA 1,535 miles

For this state we had five days for diversions before my run. We used three of them on a boat trip down the Missouri River, leaving from Fort Benton. We had a scenic drive to this town, passing wildlife and mountains under a sky that seemed so large, yet so close. When we reached Fort Benton, we stayed in the Lewis and Clark room at the Pioneer Lodge, which had numerous clippings highlighting the expedition, putting us in the "Old West" mood. Our room was comfortable, and it even came without a phone, to help put us back in time. The next morning we were ready to begin our river ride. We were traveling with the Missouri River Outfitters, whom I highly recommend if ever there is a desire to explore the upper Missouri River. Our guides and chefs for the trip were a father, mother and daughter team who knew the river and cooking well. Along the way, we stopped to

hike through cacti and yucca. Meriwether Lewis had described the
cacti as the pests of the plain as well as its beauty. We also passed hundreds of red ant hills, not a place to decide to sit and rest. At night,
our guides pitched tents for everyone on the Corps of Discovery site,
where Lewis and Clark had stopped in May of 1805. Their trip must
have been so much rougher, with no restaurants nor cars, going into
unmapped areas and no bug repellent.
Luckily they had Sacagawea, who is
carved in stone right next to them
in Fort Benton. Once the camp
was set up, Dan, a fellow
adventurer, and I decided to
take a walk. I thought it
would be interesting to get a
closer look at trees we had
seen from the boat that were
gnawed halfway through by
beavers. We headed down a path
that began at the edge of the camp
area. We had walked maybe 50 feet and
were at the beginning of the path when I heard the unmistakable
sound of a rattler. I had stepped only inches away from the long,
slithering creature. I let out a tiny, "Whoa!" and proceeded to step
back. It just so happens that our guides, Bonnie and Kyle, were
watching us. Their story differs just a little. They said something to
the effect that my tiny "Whoa!" was more like a giant "**WHOA!**" They
also mentioned something about a dance. I don't remember. I was too
busy trying to get a good photo. Anyway, I wasn't frightened a bit,
although from that point on, I let the kids lead the way on our hikes.

That night it was cool out, and we sat around the campfire
telling stories, including versions of my snake story. Two in our
group, Nancy, who insisted she didn't want to see any snakes, and
Margie, a youthful 80–year–old, had fun, giggling like teenagers.
Nancy reminded me of my oldest sister, Kathleen, because of her similar mannerisms.

The next morning, after a hearty breakfast, we traveled about
four hours in pouring rain. Despite the rain, the view was still stu-
pendous. Still, we decided to make a short day of it and stopped to

make camp. I went out for firewood, carrying a large, long log, Daniel Boone–style on my shoulder. This would make for a nice burning, long–lasting fire.

After the wood was collected, I decided to take a walk with Austin. He led the way as we started at a dried–up stream and began to follow it into the hills. We felt somewhat like Lewis and Clark as we made our way up. There was a great view looking down on the campsite, and strangely enough there was an old horse drawn plow on the very top of the hill. Dropped by airplane? Who knows? Looking back the other way, we saw a much higher mountain. Austin said he wanted to climb that, too. It was a steep and treacherous walk, but he was feeling adventurous. He was glad we were climbing together. "Dad we're finally doing a father–son thing on this trip." I beamed. Music to my ears. However, Austin was also feeling like it was time to assert himself, verbally, that is. Jeanne and I have always taught the kids that swear words are absolutely off–limits. Of course, we know the real world, and we make our share of contributions to the four–letter word exclamations on rare occasions. I'm sure Jeanne would change that "we" to "Speak for yourself, Marlin." As we continued up the steep slope, Austin, who was trying to keep his balance, was poked by a sharp cactus needle and reacted with, "Oh, *shit!*" I didn't say anything. He was quick to notice that I didn't scold or correct him on his choice of words. For some reason I realized this was important to him. We kept on walking. Austin kept trying his wings. "Watch out for them *damn* cactus." I still didn't make any corrections. Then, after some work dodging yucca, cactus and ant hills as we climbed, he said forcefully, "This is one *fuckin'* big mountain."

"Yeah, son, it is." That was all I said as we made our way to the top. When he reached the peak, he stood looking all around and down at what he had overcome on the climb. Austin was King of the Mountain. He had reached the pinnacle and perhaps his manhood, too. However far he might be behind in "common sense" and social skills, his body was taking him to manhood, and I had to respect that. The trip was four hours, but it was also a lifetime. Our trip down was a challenge, too. One slip would mean falling over cacti and ant hills. The entire trip down had a repeat of his newly–used words. We returned exhausted, ready for a nap.

The rest of the group sat around the campfire socializing, while Austin and I went to snooze. Our timing for naps couldn't have been worse. The humongous log I had carried in earlier turned out to be a good conversation piece. As the log burned in half, a very large bull snake came slithering out. It seemed to be unharmed by having been in the heat. It worked its way into the grass and moved as quickly as a snake can toward the river. Jeanne likes to create her own version of "what if" when she retells that story. "What if that bull snake came out of that log when Marlin had it on his shoulder?"

That night we all stayed up late and watched the satellites zip across the sky. Then I was awake long after they all turned in. I heard a coyote yelping from what I hoped was a far distance away. I was also up early the next morning. Debbie, Dan's wife, was already awake admiring the early dawn's beauty. After breakfast, we packed for our short ride to Judith Landing, where our river trip would end. From that point there was a scenic bus ride to Fort Benton. It had been a real pleasure to travel with this group. One of the favorites was Don Williams, an 81–year–old retired rancher. I hope that when I'm 81 I have Don's health and Margie's spirit. After we said our goodbyes, we drove to Helena, the town of the marathon. However, there was time for a little more touring before I had to run.

On Friday, we traveled to a place called the Gates of the Mountains. Marge and Nancy had convinced us it was a must–see. It was also a river ride on the Missouri River. As the boat went between the mountains, you had the impression that the mountains were opening up—a neat sight. Along the way there were mountain goats climbing above us and birds of all types flying above.

From the boat ride, we went to a ghost town that had once been a silver mining town. There we saw a sign: "You must have permission to walk in this town." Permission? Yeah, right! There was no one there to give it. We got out of the van and walked around, looking in, but not going in any buildings. The only residents we saw were groundhogs, and they didn't seem to think we needed their permission. The wind howled through the old buildings that had been deserted when the price of silver plummeted. I figured we should leave before sundown. This would be a scary place at night. Anyway, by then I was more than ready to think of the marathon. We just had time for one more quick stop, The Castle. Running through this spooky place, with its antiques, was especially fun for Erin. We wondered who had actually lived in such a home. Personally, I like our place better. Time to run and then head back to Illinois.

The Run

The marathon started in another ghost town, Marysville. Thanks to all the hiking I'd done in the past days, I was more limber for running. Also, I'd had a week to grow accustomed to the altitude. On this one, I could surely break four hours. It was a cool 35 with no wind. I could do it. I started down the first steep hill at 7 a.m., with the great pace of 6:03 for the first mile. If I could just keep this up, I'd do all right. The course continued downhill, so that my time was still under an hour for the first eight miles. Good. There was a catch, though. The downhill running was taking a toll on my quads, and I felt it. Then they had us run on gravel. About mile 11, I looked up and saw a turkey buzzard flying in circles overhead. I thought it was a little early for him, but if he came back a little later, around mile 24 or 25, he might make a meal out of me. It was starting to warm up, so I tried hard to keep the pace I had. Any less and I wouldn't even have a four–hour run. The perfect weather and scenery to look at helped. The elevation didn't seem to bother me. At the end, I pushed myself as much as I could and barely made it in less than four hours after all. I touched thumbs with the kids and greeted Jeanne. I was ready to go home. Believe it

or not, we had scheduled another marathon in a week!

Time: 3:57:47

We would have liked to have stayed longer in Montana; there was so much to see. On our way out of the state we went by Pompeys Pillar, a miniature Devil's Tower. It's named after Sacagawea's son, Pompey, and it has real proof that Clark was there. We saw where he carved his name in the stone. History seemed to be the theme of this state, as we made our last stop at Little Big Horn, where that tragic battle took place. We

watched a movie about the events there and toured the museum. There we saw numerous stones that marked the precise spots where the soldiers, and General Custer himself, were killed. At the top of the hill was a monument standing tall above the mass grave where the soldiers were buried. Custer's remains were taken to West Point. It's hard to imagine, and even more difficult to explain to

Austin and Erin, how a place that appears so peaceful was once a place of carnage and horror.

On our return home, we would inadvertently stop at a monument, still being constructed, of a man who played an important role in the events that took place at Little Big Horn (see Wyoming). After that we were ready to see modern–day Streamwood and our home before the next week's trip.

35

Dancing Jeanne
June 14, 2003

WEST VIRGINIA   566 miles

It was a 2,000 mile drive from Helena, Montana, to Williamson, West Virginia, on the other side of the country. Here, the mountains meant coal and men going under them to work. We visited the coal museum in the small town of Matewan and saw just a glimpse of how hard their lives are. We also learned of the famous feud here, that of the Hatfield and McCoy families. The nearby cemetery tells the tale of this feud.

Across the border, in nearby Pikeville, Kentucky, was the annual Hatfield and McCoy Festival. When we arrived, the main attraction was outdoor square dancing. Couples in full skirts and matching cowboy shirts were whirling around the ground to the instructions of the caller and the lively music. It reminded me of barn dances in New York when my grandfather was a caller, giving me a smile. When the music stopped, an elderly gentleman, sweating and puffing from the exercise, came over. He proudly began telling us, "You should square dance. It keeps you healthy, and the conditioning of dancing is greater than that from running." He was very sure of himself as he continued with his dissertation that put down running. It lasted at least 10 minutes, or up until the point where he asked about us. Jeanne explained that we were from Chicago, and I was there to run in a marathon—26.2 miles. Seeing that we had put him in an awkward moment, I assured him he was right, and that he and his fellow dancers would certainly do well in any marathon.

Before long, he was dancing again, about the same time I figured we needed to go. I got up to get the kids, who were playing nearby. I returned to find Jeanne up and dancing with the group. One of the gentlemen, who had been eyeballing her for quite some time, took advantage of my short absence and invited her to join in. I must say, she caught on very well. Of course, she did give me a peculiar look, and if I read her mind correctly, she was thinking, "I'm going to get you back for this." They did try to rope me into it, too, but I decided it wouldn't be right for a runner to show these dancers a thing or two. After all, the next day was the reenactment of the end of the feud. I wanted to keep peace in the town. I'd stick to running.

The Run

The neat thing about this run was that the runners were divided into two groups, designated the Hatfields and the McCoys. When the run was completed, the total times of all the runners would be calculated, and the group with the fastest time would be declared the winner of the feud for that year. I was designated a McCoy. The race director, David, was a true Hatfield. He put on a first–class event that I was glad to be part of. After a small speech by David, the groups were off. The first part of the course wound through Kentucky before coming back to the West Virginia side. Early on, the miles of driving and lack of activity the week before was evident. In the first mile, I barely broke eight minutes. By mile six, I wasn't breaking, I was averaging eight minutes. Then there was a mile–long hill that I struggled up as others passed me. At the top, just past mile seven, there was another steep downhill. I sprinted down feeling like a McCoy being chased by a Hatfield with a shotgun. I was loose and moving quickly. My quads

were absorbing the hard impacts, but I was on a roll. I even passed about 20 other runners. I wished I could have run like this in Albuquerque. I did that mile in under six minutes, but after that, when things flattened out, I never broke eight minutes per mile the rest of the way. So, during these slower miles, I made it a point to observe my surroundings. On my left, there was a small creek, and every so often there was a small house or trailer on the other side. One would have to cross some rickety bridges made of railroad ties, corrugated tin roofing and tree branches to get across. I watched a large car noisily struggle across one, wondering if it were even going to make it, and being amazed that it did.

A little farther on, I reached down and pet a dog that was just behind another runner. He started to follow me, and after that, everyone thought he was mine. He tagged along for about four miles until I asked a spectator to hold him back.

A little bit past the halfway point, I crossed a bouncy, swinging bridge that was a little weird. It wasn't long after that when the heat and my quads started to take their toll. I felt defeated, as I knew four hours was no longer realistic. Oh well, it still felt good to see Austin first, then Jeanne and Erin cheering me to the finish at the famous Coal House. (A house literally made out of coal.) I guess I don't have to make 4 hours every time. Besides, as I later learned, we McCoys won. Hurray for us!

Time: 4:30:45

36

Living A Charmed Life
August 24, 2003

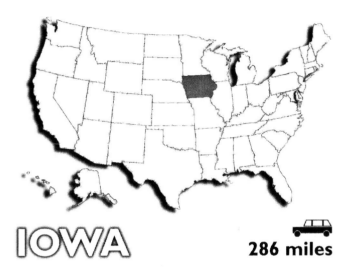

IOWA   286 miles

After the Hatfield–McCoy run, I started doing something I had not done since Hawaii—logging my training. MarathonGuide.com is an excellent site for marathon runners. It has a member login, where members can keep track of their progress in a personal log. You put in all the information, and it calculates the results in a variety of ways. After I reviewed my July and August results, it was evident that I wasn't doing enough training. I really didn't need a Web site or computer to tell me that. I knew, and my body knew. My work and family always had to come first. This run was no exception. In the month of August, including the Iowa marathon, I ran seven times. I just didn't have the time for more. For the three weeks before Iowa, I had a 19–day stretch with no days off work. Add to that poor Erin started having asthma attacks in the middle of the night. Scary, very scary.

Jeanne and I had difficulty going back to sleep after the nervous time of these attacks. Well, it would be nice for us all to be relaxed outdoors, camping in fresh air, out under the stars again. From RunnersWorld.com, I selected this run in Fairfield, Iowa. It didn't have a medal, which was very important to us, and which I had received in every other run. They hang on my living room wall as reminders of all our shared experiences. They are a joy for us to look at. Also, this was a trail run, and I knew my limited training would make it a difficult challenge. Regardless of all this, we would go to Iowa. Actually, this was the fourth time I signed up to run in Iowa. Conflicts, including the tragic loss of my brother–in–law Ed in 2002, kept me from running an earlier marathon.

Now was my time to run this state. I worked Saturday morning from 5 a.m. to about 11:15, hoping to leave sooner to spend as much time as possible in Iowa. Jeanne took the van to have it cleaned, but I asked her not to fill it with gas. We'd find better prices away from Chicago. It had a quarter–tank, which should get us quite far away. So we had a quick lunch at the Old Country Buffet and headed west. The goal was to be at the camp site by 5 p.m. As I sped along, I kept an eye on the gas gauge. When the Windstar is at a quarter tank, there are six more gallons, about 150 more miles. So when Jeanne noticed the low fuel light on, she looked over. "Are you going to stop at the next exit?" "No. Let's cross the Mississippi River and get into Iowa first."

She looked out the window and didn't say anything else, but then her eyes kept wandering back to the gauge. We crossed the river, and I noticed a gas station sign way off in the distance. It was not an easy–off, easy–on exit, so I pushed a little further. Then I saw the next sign: "Davenport, 16 miles." Trouble was on the way. It came 10 miles later, when the van just died. I let it coast as far as it could, which happened to be right at a rest stop. How lucky? Jeanne got out her AAA card, and I made the call. Thanks, Fran, at AAA, for your help. So then we just waited. Austin and I went exploring and then played catch with an old tennis ball. In 30 minutes we had two gallons of gas. The man said, "You're in AAA. There's no charge." I put a 20 in his hand anyway, on condition he not tell any of my friends. I should have given it to Jeanne instead, so *she* wouldn't tell anyone. When we got back home, she couldn't tell enough people of how "I tried to tell him." Then she went on to say, "You live a charmed life,

Marlin, because if it had been me, I would have been 20 or more miles away from a rest stop." *Regardless of whether or not I live a "charmed life," I still have to endure the humiliation of admitting, at least this time, that Jeanne was right. "Man that was tough!"* At 6:30 p.m. we were in the park in Iowa and pitching our tent. We invited the man camping next to us to come over for marshmallows and hot dogs. It turned out Albert was a runner, too, so, of course, we exchanged long stories of our marathons. We rested a little. Then the coughing came from Erin in her own little tent. Fear always comes with these attacks. It was very late before we were all asleep.

The Run

In the early dawn, Albert and I made the short walk to the starting area. It was just a few minutes past 7 a.m. when the gun went off, and we headed down the well–maintained trail under a canopy of trees. We had to travel twists and turns, up hill and down hill, on soft ground and over stones—all the challenges a course could offer. I proceeded with caution and what pace was possible. There were no mile markers, but when I saw a water stand, I figured I was at the halfway around the loop mark. The good part was that the course circled around, so I was never more than a couple of miles from our camp site at any time. I got to see Jeanne and the kids at least ten times during the run, my favorite part. I thoroughly enjoyed completing each loop. When I approached the starting area each time, the score keepers and spectators would call out my name. "Way to go, Marlin!" "Keep it up, Marlin!" This got my motors running, and I called out updates on my progress. After the second round, I was having a feeling of déjà vu. The scorekeeper would circle a number on his sheet to keep track of each runner's progress. By my fifth turn, I tried to convince him this was actually my sixth, that I went so fast he missed me on my last trip. No dice. His quick reply was, "Two IDs and a check. I'm not cheap."

Geez, I left my checkbook in the tent.

I was enjoying the run with all the people around cheering, but I wasn't making that good a time. I passed the halfway line in two hours. I'd never break four hours on this one. It was getting hot, but I didn't stop for water. Then, about the 15th mile, I came down a hill, and my right foot hit something, and I tumbled down. Splat! I got up dirty, with a bloody left knee and a throbbing big right toe. I had to stop. I walked over to a picnic table near a water stop and took off my shoe. There was a swollen black and blue big right toe. I thought for sure it was broken. It hurt terribly. Jeanne came over to check it out and offer sympathy. I was faced with my first DNF (did not finish) decision. I dwelled on it for about 15 minutes. Would I stop, or would I not? Then, tenderly, I put my sock and shoe back on and stood up. Even if I had to walk the next 10 miles, I *would* complete the run. Just as I rose, another runner, Pat, came up and said she was walking with a little running. I figured I'd just hang out with her, so I started out. Even walking was excruciatingly painful, so I tried to take my mind off it by talking with Pat. She was inspiring. At 53, she quit smoking and started to run. Now she was 56 and looked 45. After a while, I realized my toe was going to hurt like the dickens anyway, so I might as well run. I crossed the start line for the fifth time right at four hours. The hot, stubborn sun entered the equation and made me nauseated, but I'm stubborn, too. I moved forward and crossed the finish line in just over five hours.

Time: 5:03:05

My finish time was depressing, but at least I would not have a DNF on my record, and I had received so much down–home friendliness and good will, that memories of Iowa will always be positive. Our friend, Albert, even stayed around to help me take down the tent. I'd go home and create my own medal. There were two months for my toe to heal before New Hampshire.

37

The Setup
October 4, 2003

NEW HAMPSHIRE 1,102 miles

I chose to drive, instead of flying to New Hampshire, as I wanted to throw in Connecticut, and after that, I had schemed a plot for a surprise detour. So, right after work Thursday, we were on the tollway. By the next day we were in Utica, NY, to visit my Uncle Walt and Aunt Joyce. Whenever relatives are in a state we pass, I try to take advantage of it, because family is what this life is all about. Austin and Erin need that connection to other generations, as do we. While there, I showed Walt our planned route of travel that included a return drive through Pennsylvania. Walt told us that a cousin of his, named Mary Ellen, lived in Pennsylvania, raised popcorn and, coincidently, lived very near the interstate we would be traveling on. That did it. Jeanne is a connoisseur of popcorn. It's our nighttime staple as we watch TV. To sweeten the pot, he also added that Mary Ellen wanted to read my stories of the marathons. An incentive for each of us. We would certainly make a detour to Mary's on the drive home. We'd even get extra for the stop at Jeanne's parents on the return.

More than popcorn, Jeanne loves dogs. We had all suffered with the passing of Fuzz, but our plans of a greyhound didn't work out. So all summer, instead of pestering me for her replacement ring, Jeanne instead pushed, "Let's get a dog." I had answered with good excuses and lame ones for why we shouldn't get one. Austin and Erin sided with me because they were happy with their two new kittens, Laka and Hula (Hawaiian names). Jeanne did not give up. She spent time on petfinder.com, determined to find one. She probably would someday. But for now, she was content with the promise of future popcorn, as we drove on to Bristol. There, we were lucky enough to be guests of Continental 737 Captain Steve and his wife Betty, who extended great hospitality instead of us having to stay in an impersonal hotel. The dog discussion was tabled for the time being, but I knew it would be back. For now, all my concentration was on the marathon.

The Run

Steve drove me to the starting line under a cool, overcast sky. He said he'd stay as a volunteer, working a ham radio. I went on to get my number. I heard some 50 State Club members saying they were going to run in Maine the next day, and I was jealous. Even though I had, what I consider, high mileage in training runs, 110 miles in September, I knew it wasn't enough for me to do back–to–back marathons. I would just focus on this one, rationalizing why I was there.

The starting horn went off, and I forgot the "why" and ran. The course went around Newfound Lake, under the colorful fall foliage. I just relaxed and made a 7:45 first mile. Despite the beauty, the course was not really good for runners. It went along a busy highway. Fortunately, the drivers were courteous and drove around us, but to avoid running on an uneven surface, you had to run in the middle of the road. I chose to run at an angle, which gave me a sore left knee. Marathons are painful for anyone who "guts it out," but I felt more pain just watching another runner. He was running it barefoot! My feet cringed at the thought, but kept going, and I came in under four hours with another nonstopper. Betty and Steve were there to help Jeanne, Austin and Erin welcome me to the finish line.

Time: 3:56:08

Steve and Betty did even more for us than offer their home and volunteer. After the race, they invited us to visit their neighbors, Nadine and Glenn. There, the kids saw llamas and horses, as well as dogs, cats and sheep. One of the sheep, Tamale, was once an Illinois resident. I helped her get out here, where she happily gave birth to two more. She also gives generously of her wool, which Nadine uses on her loom to make colorful blankets. It was a trip back to the time of early New Hampshire, but with all the modern conveniences. It was also a chance for the kids to do some farm chores, hearing again of Dad's "good old days on the farm." They especially liked the llamas, with their long necks. Erin and I watched one of them eat some hay. It chewed a bit and then swallowed. As it swallowed, we could see a lump travel down the length of its neck. Erin looked up with surprise

and tried to describe what she had just seen. It was funny because she was excited about what she had just seen, but she couldn't get any words out to describe it. She just pointed at the llama, laughing, and made some indiscernible sounds to get our attention, "Uh, uh, uh." We all had to watch it again and laugh with her. It was comical to see. We enjoyed watching her excitement. These marathons have brought Austin and Erin a double lifetime of experiences in just a few years.

After we left the farm, there was more touring time. This time we went up Rattlesnake Mountain, where we could see the lake where "On Golden Pond" was filmed. Then, on Monday, we tried another mountain, Mount Washington, the highest in the northeast. It once had winds blowing 256 mph in 1934! The snow kept us from going to the summit, but we made it to the tree line, listening to a guide on a CD. When the CD was over, the topic switched from mountain scenery to dogs. How did that happen? Perhaps Jeanne saw a dog along the road or remembered the dogs at Nadine's farm. Well, it doesn't take much to start the subject. This time it was, "What do you want to name our next dog?" I didn't really want another dog, but one would surely arrive sometime. "Why not a Hawaiian name, like the cats?" "No, we're naming our next dog Popcorn." Of course she had mentioned this as an idea for a name a couple of times already. This time she was more sure of herself. "Ha!" I said, and smiled to myself. The choice of names made my secret things much more inter-

esting. Right then, I tried to steer the conversation to the sights we were going to see the next day. And they were fun. We saw Lost River Gorge, where you squeeze through tight crevices of granite boulders created by glaciers. Then we went on a gondola ride up Cannon Mountain. We arrived at the same time as two busloads of senior English ladies and were all packed in so tight we could hardly see out. Suddenly, I felt a too–friendly pinch of my backside. I thought Jeanne was

getting away with a quick move, but I turned to see that Jeanne was way on the other side. I wondered which of those little old ladies had a secret. We were happy to get off that ride and back on our own. We stopped in the narrow Flume Gorge, but at least we were in this tight spot with just ourselves. On the way we passed the "Old Man of the Mountain," a symbol of New Hampshire. Unfortunately, nature had eroded what looked like a man's profile, but people still honor the mountain. We ended the trip with a return to Betty and Steve's, where, in the spirit of the upcoming Halloween, we carved pumpkins and toasted the seeds. Austin ate most of them, which made him sick on our drive to Connecticut. He filled the van with gas so bad we had to stop and air it out. Gasp! Choke! We all walked around to breathe a little fresh air before getting back in.

Topping this, Erin was belligerent on this drive, saying things she didn't usually say, angry at the world in general. It was just time to get us all to our Connecticut hotel for some R&R.

38

Popcorn, Anyone?
November 11, 2003

CONNECTICUT 923 miles

In this state I had to read my email. Actually, Walt's suggestion for us to stop for popcorn was my idea. It was a special "popcorn." I had been sending emails to Mary Ellen all along, but Walt played along with the gag, presenting the idea as his. Now I had to hook up my laptop and check the email and see if she were ready for our visit. She was supposed to email us an invitation to her house. Unfortunately, I was unable to get online at the hotel. So we stopped at a couple of libraries, on the pretense that I needed more information on the marathon. (I had already sent a note to Mary Ellen that Jeanne would be reading all my email.) I tried the libraries, but I couldn't get connected. I'd have to find another way to communicate with her.

In the meantime, on to sightseeing. The first stop was Mark Twain's home and a well–guided tour telling us all about Tom Sawyer

and Huckleberry Finn. Then it was on to a clock museum that the literature described as "interactive." Good. We went in and looked at clocks of all styles and shapes and listened to audio tapes. In the basement, we saw large clocks with pendulums, and Austin was learning physics in action by pushing one. I had just played with the same old, expensive clock he was touching, but he received a sharp reprimand. "Don't touch that!" Then we saw that all the displays had signs that said the same: "Do not touch." We hadn't seen them before. We moved quickly out of the museum. Outside, Jeanne wondered aloud, "Exactly what does interactive mean?" Good question. Time for a meal break. The runner's packet described a downtown restaurant with runner's pasta. Okay. We'd try that. We did, but it was undercooked and overpriced. The kids didn't like theirs, and the total bill, including parking, was $70. So much for being frugal. Well, you can't always tell by looking at a place. I was ready for bed.

The Run

I was at the start an hour and a half early in the morning cold, trying to talk myself into the marathon. The announcer said it was the biggest sporting event in the state of Connecticut. I had to admit it felt good to be a part of this. The gun went off, and so did I. I had a decent sub eight-minute pace going for a while. I wanted a non-stopper, but nature had other ideas, so I hit the bushes, which were plentiful around us. As I jumped back in the group the 3:30 pacer passed us. I wasn't having any trouble following him. Then, about the 11th mile, I felt the tightness coming on. I was struggling to keep up, getting slower and slower. The main difference on this run compared to all the others was my thought process. I had a secret that I needed to hold onto for one more day, and it kept my mind busy, helping me pass each mile.

Just shy of four hours, I was greeted by Jeanne and the kids, but oh, boy, was I sore! Nice medal, though. Not bad. I had gone through 12 marathons in 12 months. Not bad for a guy who, in 2000, had only run one. I had 37 states plus D.C. I didn't stay around admiring my medal long, though. We had miles to go.

Time: 3:54:44

We headed out to Springville, Pennsylvania, to visit my Uncle Raymond and Aunt Judy, the same ones who watched me run in Harrisburg. On the way I took a wrong turn, and we passed a sign that read, "Free puppies." Did Jeanne need any more reminders? Reaching our relatives' farm, we had time for chores and a chicken dinner. Jeanne kept mentioning, though, the next day the Chicago Cubs were in the playoffs, and she wanted to be at her parents' home in Dayton to watch the game.

"I'm sorry. I'm not sure we can make it. I just called Mary Ellen for directions, and she's expecting us." I had called to make sure all systems were go, since email hadn't worked out. "Let's leave right after breakfast, at least, so we have a better chance of seeing some of the game."

We did, but I could tell Jeanne was wishing we didn't have to visit someone's cousin. When I was close by, I was a little unsure, so I stopped to call. Jeanne was getting anxious and sending me some nonverbal signals to hurry. Finally, we were in Mary Ellen's driveway. There, I acted like the visit was to share stories and took out a copy of my marathon book. After a little bit of artificial socializing, I looked over at Mary Ellen. "By the way, Uncle Walt said not to leave here without Popcorn." Jeanne came more to life. The detour had merit if we were going to load up on popcorn. "Yes. I'll be right back," Mary Ellen answered. In a minute she was back and, to Jeanne's delight, coming right to her, was a large, very soft and friendly puppy. "Awww," was all Jeanne could say as she bent to hug the dog as it licked her. Then Austin and Erin came out and were all over this excited pup. This dog was a winner. During all the excitement, Mary Ellen announced the dog was a Bernese Mountain Dog, and she was a breeder who raised them. Austin thought that was a cool job and asked, "Are you jealous, Mom?'

Jeanne replied with a, "Yes, I am jealous," in a sort of weak, squeaky, emotional voice. Then Mary Ellen interjected, "You will be more jealous, Jeanne, because this one's name is Popcorn"

Now Jeanne was thinking to herself, "That's what we plan on naming our next dog." So she responded to Mary Ellen by saying, "No way!" Mary Ellen then said, "Yes, way, and she's yours."

I just sat and glowed because I knew I had scored some big points. We then went to the barn to meet Popcorn's mother, and I knew then we had the right dog. When we went back out, I was surprised to see Erin crying. Jeanne went to comfort her. "I'm not sad, Mom. I'm just so happy we have a dog." Then Jeanne had a few questions of her own. "Is Walt really your cousin?" "No." "Do you even know him?" "Well, we have emailed each other a couple of times." "So you don't even grow popcorn?' Mary Ellen shook her head. "No."

"So how long have you two been planning this?" "About a couple of months now." Jeanne squeezed my hand. "Thanks, Marlin."

Time to hit the road for home.

We did stop, of course, at Jeanne's parents' home on the way. Naturally, Popcorn was the family hit. She even peed on their carpet. I never said anything about the cost of this special dog. Ironically, just a few days before, there was a check from an annuity fund of Jeanne's departed Aunt Virginia that turned out to be the same amount as the cost of the dog. Coincidence?

39

This Sucks, But I Have Good News
November 9, 2003

MARYLAND 720 miles

About the only attraction we saw in Maryland was the movie "Pirates of The Caribbean" on the hotel television. We had to fly in, let me run, and fly out. But I wanted to complete 13 marathons in 13 months, so I would only have 13 more to go. With all these numbers, Austin added that he, too, was 13, an age to appreciate these trips, except for this one. Also, Bethesda is right by Washington D.C., and we had already had a great visit to those sights. The time was so short because of our compressed work schedules. It's always a risk with the standby flights we want to get on, but we made it. The only detail was that the rental car agency gave us a Jeep instead of the car we asked for, but travelers get used to that. We assured the kids that we only had 20 miles to go in the Jeep before the hotel. However, the trip took two hours because of traffic and difficult directions. They were glad to unpack, find a steakhouse, and settle in front of the pirates.

The Run

Jeanne took me to the starting line early, so I had time to do too much thinking about why I was doing this and how I'd prefer to be home in bed. Maybe I should arrive a second before the gun goes off, so I wouldn't think so much. I thought to myself, "this really sucks". If one could have observed me standing there waiting, they would have seen a stern frustrated look on my face suddenly change with a raise of my right eyebrow to a look of pleasant satisfaction. I had good news. I was here in Bethesda. This was the home of the GEICO insurance company. This was the land of my low–cost insurance. As in their commercials, everything was going to be OK, and I got myself ready to start. My body warmed up quickly as I started running under clear skies. I had heard that the year before, the runners were hit by a downpour, like my New Jersey run, but this day was perfect. I ran up and down the rolling hills and past some inquisitive deer. I also kept in mind that our flight left at noon, so I'd make this a nonstopper, if possible. It was. I rushed across the finish to greet the family, collect my medal and keep going in our private marathon to the hotel. Like a family being chased by crooks in a movie, we dashed to our Jeep and started out to the airport. However, in movies they always know their way, and the traffic moves out of the way. Not so for us. We had wrong turns and heavy traffic, but just in time we turned in the un–requested Jeep and dashed to the security check. I don't know how we did it, but we were soon up, up and away, with Maryland far below.

Time: 3:40:58

40

So Close
February 21, 2004

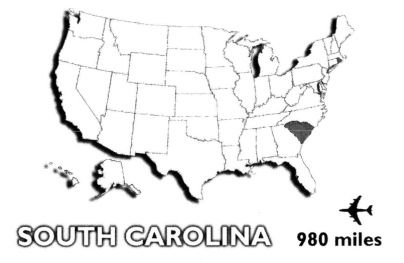

SOUTH CAROLINA   ✈ 980 miles

The Maryland run turned out to be my best performance in all of 2003. It gave me good hopes for 2004, so I set myself some ambitious goals for training. I was determined to make my next run qualify me for Boston.

With that in mind, I ran 109 miles in December, taking Popcorn with me. She loved to run. One morning, it was freezing cold, about 20 degrees, with hundreds of geese gathered at a nearby lake. Since it was 3 a.m. and no one was around, I decided to let Popcorn loose and let her run with the wind, her own training. However, she saw the geese and dashed off toward the lake, which was only partially frozen. As she approached the sloped bank by the shore, she tried to put her doggy brakes on. It was like watching a cartoon. She hit the ice, her rear going down and her front legs standing up. She slid ten feet right into the icy water. Splash! I rushed toward her, but she made her way out with ease, like the frisky puppy she was. She tried to shake off the water, but it was freezing on her. When we were home she ran right upstairs and jumped in bed with Jeanne, icicles and all. After that, I tried to continue my training, but the weather wasn't having any of it. One day, it was 12 degrees at noon, with a windchill factor of zero. The run was slow and very rough on my knees. There was one saving grace. Jeanne won a month's fitness center pass at her office Christmas party. I used it six times, going round and round a track that had nine laps to the mile. It was warm, all right, but I couldn't stand running just in a circle. I did enough to be able, I hoped, to break four hours in Myrtle Beach, and not an inch more. I was ready. Time to fly. U.S. Airways gave us some non–rev passes. We waited in the airport, but it was another close call. The only reason we made it on the first flight out was that 12 vacationers going to the Cayman Islands didn't have the proper documents to travel. Our names were called, and we took off for Charlotte, North Carolina. Close, but not there yet. We were bumped off two more flights to Myrtle Beach. Despite this, we still arrived in time to enjoy a warm, sunny afternoon walk on the beach with a stop at Ripley's Believe It or Not. Then we went back to the hotel, so I could toss and turn and be nervous in bed, worrying about the run.

The Run

I shared a taxi with an Ohio lady who was running the half–marathon. We arrived at the start to see thousands of people milling around, talking and stretching. They were preparing for the marathon, a half–marathon and a relay marathon. Myrtle Beach was packed, but it's a city that likes crowds and excitement. Tourists are its daily bread. Once the gun went off, it didn't take long to get past the morning chill on this very flat course. I moved along at a chipper pace, seven–and–a–half minutes per mile. After the first hour, however, my legs began to protest. They had rehearsed just enough for one hour. I explained that there were three other hours. They didn't listen. I tried to just "gut it out," thinking of having fun with the family afterward. Then, at about the 17th mile, I passed the time talking to a runner from Wisconsin for about six miles. When he started to

back down, I noticed my pain more and knew it would be a tight
squeeze to break four hours. Just before the 25th mile, we had to turn
and run the other way. The wind that had been at my back was now
coming straight into me. This was going to be tough. At least it was
going to be another run without stopping. That's all I could say for
it. I crossed the finish in just *over* four hours. It was very disappointing to me to be 'so close' to breaking four hours but at least I'd added
another state. Now we'd see the place.
Time: 4:00:23

We chose Ripley's Aquarium as our sight to see beyond the
beach. Good choice. We rode a moving sidewalk while it traveled
through an acrylic tunnel. All kinds of sea life, including sharks and
sawfish, came over to look at us. They looked relaxed and peaceful,
swimming around wondering why we were out of water. We bid
them goodbye because we had a plane to catch. Actually, we had to
sit for hours in airports while we were bumped off flights before we
finally made it home to freezing Chicago. A marathon had taken us
to warmth. I'd look for warmth again in March.

41

First Across the Line
March 20, 2004

CALIFORNIA 2,204 miles

The stage was set for stress from the beginning. Jeanne rushed home from work, and we rushed to get the kids from school in time to be at O'Hare at 5 p.m. We made it. Yahoo! Oops, not yahoo. The flight was full, so we were bumped. There were 10 other non–revs with seniority over us. For the first time, I felt just a little bitter about my involuntary downgrade from management to agent a year ago. As a manager, I would have had priority over the other non–revs. As all of the major carriers were doing, Continental was trying to trim its budget, and it started with management. I was lowest in seniority, so I was one of the first to experience an 18% cut in pay. Ouch! My job responsibilities did not change. I was like a ghost manager receiving an agent's pay. Although I was a little frustrated that day, I clearly understood the necessity of the cut and accepted it.

The result was we had to just wait. We were getting used to that in our travels. I decided it was time to dip into our travel funds and eat at the Airport Hilton restaurant. At least I had a 25% employee discount. After the meal, we waited some more. If we didn't get on the next one, I wouldn't be able to run on Saturday. The flight was four hours late, but we were on it, and headed to Houston. (Not direct, but the price was right.) The next morning we were on our way to San Jose, the closet place to San Miguel with hotel rooms available. When I went to pick up my packet, the race director, Eileen, stated that the runners could start with the walkers at 6:30 a.m. because of the abnormal high temperatures. Great. I did want that. The second "great" came when I ran into marathon legend Wally Herman and got an autograph. He had not started running until he retired from work, but he had run 640 marathons! After getting his signature, Eileen's husband was nice enough to give us a tour of the course in nearby Camp Roberts Army Base. The only flat parts were the first and last miles. The brochure said it wasn't a course to set a personal record. The drive left me with a little dread. My knees were sore from straining them at work. It was going to be a cloudless hot day, and my pre–run training was only nine miles. This wasn't going to be good. At least I had the vacation part after the run to look forward to. Then Eileen's husband invited us to the pasta dinner for runners at a school. I was glad to go, because all the profits would go to that school. People like Eileen and her husband and her assistant, Linda, are the backbone of the races, the true heroes of our society. I felt their energy and sincerely admired their teaching of the values of good health to the kids.

The Run

Since I was going to start so early, we left the kids at the hotel and Jeanne drove me. It was a gorgeous morning for a run, under a clear sky. At the start, I saw there were ten runners starting early. This included a husband–wife pair and Wally Herman. Eileen called, "Get on your marks. Get set. Go." We were off. In a short while I realized I was ahead of the others. Okay, so I was the junior runner of the group, but I could still enjoy the glory of the moment. Not acknowledging the real facts allowed me to feel I was going at a blazing speed. At about three miles I looked back and didn't see anyone. I

was actually by myself. I wondered how long this would last. This was an unimaginably neat feeling I was experiencing. I was in first place in a marathon! Usually, by the second half of a race, runners are speeding by me, and I imagine they are chuckling to themselves over their little victories. I tried not to think about what my position was, rather just concentrate on mile after mile and the scenery. There was a giant frog in the road and herds of sheep on each side. The trees were full of squirrels. It was good to be alive, to be in this place, at this time, regardless of running positions. I reached mile 14 in under two hours. It was 8:30 and the others were just starting the run. I felt guilty about them. (Not!) I passed my closest competitor going the other way at mile 15, the wife of the couple team, as I had made the turn point and was on my way back. I might come in first if I kept up my pace. The heat was becoming a factor, and at miles 20, 22, and 24, I stopped at a water table and poured water on my head and aching calves. I was carrying Gatorade to drink. Still, muscle spasms began, and my last mile took 15 minutes.

For my second run in a row, I did not break four hours. However, I was just happy to finish and see Jeanne, Austin and Erin cheering for me. And for the first time in my life, I crossed the finish line before any other marathoner. I didn't take first place, though. There were three other runners who left at 8:30 who had better times than I did. I figured that if they were running in more heat, their air was thinner and offered less resistance. I was running in thicker air. (That sounds logical, right?) Another first was that I had a terrific massage. Usually the lines are too long. The massage prevented the usual pain I have after runs.

Time: 4:16:57

After the massage, it was time to think only of enjoying ourselves. We did it in style. We drove east to a Best Western Hotel at the foot of the Sierra Nevada Mountains just outside of Sequoia National Park. Along the way we saw proof that California is a garden state. We saw orange, peach and olive trees, as well as vegetable gardens. At

night we ate in an outdoor restaurant under the stars, savoring the place and each other.

Sunday morning, it was time to look for the giant sequoia tree, General Sherman. We found him, and many more, unbelievably gigantic. As we drove higher, the trees just got taller and wider around. We drove up to 7,000 feet. There, we marveled at these

ancient living things that had been around thousands of years. One that had fallen in the 1950s had rings that dated back to B.C. So much happened in the world while that tree was here in that forest, growing with its friends. We learned about how man is polluting and destroying these forests. When will we learn? We left still in awe of what we'd seen.

Down on flat land, we visited my oldest sister, Kathleen. There, Austin and Erin played with their cousins Leah and Emily on the beach. What a treat to be out of cold Chicago and with extended family. Socializing is easier for our kids with guaranteed friends like cousins. California is so large, it's like two states. We took time to see the most we could, leaving the next day for San Francisco. There, we arrived five minutes late for our planned boat trip to Alcatraz, but since we are a patient lot, we waited as "standbys" for the next one. We're used to being standbys. We just made it. The week before we had seen, "Escape From Alcatraz," so the kids were familiar with the place.

Coming back, since we're in such good shape, we rented tandem bikes and rode to the end of the Golden Gate Bridge and back. I had Erin, and she seemed to pedal backwards on the uphills. (UGH!) Jeanne let Austin be the front rider on the drive out, which she said she would never do again. She feared for her life as he drove on both sides of the path and sped down the hills. On the bridge, she let out an, "AYYYYYYYY!" when she discovered how high up the bridge really was. She was just in a hurry to get safely back. We still got in a couple of pictures and headed for another harrowing ride, up and down the streets of San Francisco, where stop signs leave you hanging halfway up a hill.

We were going to see a musical, and we made it just in time to park and sprint to the theater. Giving the usher our tickets, we stopped to catch our breath. He had a surprise for us. "Sorry. Your tickets are for tomorrow." "What?" Jeanne is always so efficient on reservations and plans that I couldn't say anything. We wouldn't be there tomorrow, but the usher found us some vacant seats way at the top and we enjoyed "Mama Mia!" with the others. Then it was back to visit my sister, where she and I had some discussions of our own mama. That's a story we may never understand. We have struggled to make some sense of our childhood and have only come to the conclusion that this is our reality, so we live with it and go on from there. That's all anyone can do. I have my own family now, and that's the most important fact.

I got the dear ones up before dawn, how to be unpopular, but I wanted to catch one of the 14 flights out of San Francisco that day. Surely there would be one with four spaces. There was, but it took us across the country to Newark, from where we flew back to Chicago. Total, 15 hours. We could have flown around the world, I believe. Standby non–rev tickets are for the birds. (Even they wouldn't want to wait that long to migrate.) The vote was unanimous: Next time we drive. Once we returned, I learned that I was reinstated as a manager with all my pay back. Yahoo!

42

Austin is Taller Than I Am
May 16, 2004

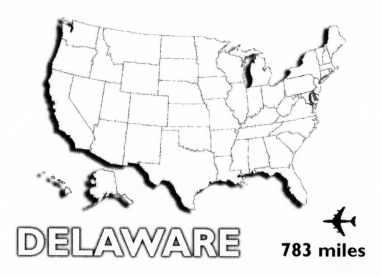

DELAWARE   783 miles

Well, we didn't keep our resolve. We flew to Delaware. Due to work
and school, we didn't have enough time for anything else. So there we
were again, in a mile-long line waiting to hear our names called.
Looking around, I noticed something that must have happened
overnight. Austin was now taller than I was. I had him stand right up
next to me, and he saw it, too. "I'm taller, Dad." "I know. You're
growing up." I was thinking of all the implications that came with
that. He was getting taller, but getting older would bring with it so
many more changes. I was glad it was just height right now. He is still
a kid for a while longer, and we would be enjoying more trips together. As I looked at him, I remembered it was just a few days before that
I had attended an Individualized Educational Plan, or IEP, meeting
at Austin's school to map out his MLP (Modified Learning Program)

for high school. It was hard to imagine that my son was going to be a freshman next year. There were ten people participating, including a social worker, psychologist, a school supervisor and his current teacher. It was the first meeting for which Jeanne was not able to attend. That was too bad because it was one of the most positive meetings yet. Austin had been making leaps and bounds in his academic progress, and everyone had very nice comments about him. However, the best part came when his teacher, Mrs. Pederson, gave her review. She identified his strengths and weaknesses and reinforced the fact that he had to remain in an MLP because he was still at a level way below his age group. Then she concluded with the statement that, "Austin's greatest asset is his family." She elaborated a little on the great value he was receiving from the real–life experiences of the family trips. I left that meeting feeling so good that when I got to work I bought everyone pizza that night.

Children with Asperger's Syndrome (AS) often want to stick to repetitive routines, yet we, on our own, had taken them out of routine and let them discover the world, and, with it, themselves. They have trouble with social interaction, and we had taken them to meet unknown relatives and put them in social situations as tourists, and it had worked out as a benefit. As parents, we were also being their guides and teachers in life. So it was with a new pride in knowing I was doing the right thing that I waited with Austin, Erin and Jeanne in the airport for a flight to Philadelphia. After a while, we did get out that day, and it was a short drive down to Wilmington. Would Austin be asking someday if he could drive? Common sense is such an important part of driving. Unfortunately, that's what he has the most trouble with. For now, he was glad to just hit the hotel pool with Erin and be himself, having fun, while I went for my runner's packet. This marathon was special because it was the only certified course in the state. It was also a 50 State Club marathon reunion run, so I found myself with the elite of endurance. The one difference I saw between these people and me was, and is, they enjoy the running. I carried my scrapbook with me in hopes of picking up another autograph, and I did. It was from Nancy Broadbridge. In 1997, she and her husband completed the 50 states in one calendar year! Their experience can be read on the Web and is called "Married to the Marathon." This was her 166th run!

We met more 50 States Club runners at the Saturday evening
pasta party dinner. Speeches were made, trophies handed out and
achievements acknowledged. Two runners, Lois Berkowitz and Alan
Steggles, would be running their 200th marathon the next day. While
watching these people get recognized, I gave my applause, but I was
thinking that the only way I would run more than 50 states would be
to get paid for it.

The Run

   I found my friend Layne at the start area on Sunday morning. He
enlightened me with his 50–mile experience from the week before. I
was feeling normal and thinking the people around me were nuts. I
guess everyone has his or her motivations. The morning air was
humid, but a few sprinkles were falling already. The course was four
loops around the Wilmington River front. Some runners like this
type of run because they can see their friends on the loop. It's also easier for planners because there are fewer aid stations. I personally
detest this type of course. They have an adverse psychological effect
on me. I get around once and I say to myself, "I have to do this shit
again?" Now you know what I was thinking on this course. Plus, I
wasn't interested in seeing how well my friends were doing. Layne,
who was over 50, was blowing me away. This was more humiliating
than inspiring. The morning became hotter, and so did I. Despite
this, I did all right through 22 miles. Then the heat was really getting
to me. By mile 24, I was sick and not sure if I was going to make it.
All I had to do was to hold to ten minute miles to break four hours.
But that sun just kept beating down on me, and I was feeling really
bad. I stared at the ground and shuffled as best I could. I knew four
hours was no longer realistic. The only thing I could do was complete
it nonstop, so I forced myself on. I stumbled across the finish and,
without even acknowledging Jeanne and the kids, fell onto the grass.
Waves of nausea swept over me, and I couldn't move.
Time: 4:07:15

   Within an hour I felt a little better and ready to see Delaware
after a cool shower. We didn't know where we wanted to go, so we
started toward Dover to see what the state had. About halfway, we

stopped at a visitors' center. The attendant told us about an air show at the Dover Air Force Base.

"That's where I worked two weeks during Desert Storm," I had to tell the attendant, who'd heard it all. "Thanks for the tip about the show."

We watched the Blue Angels fly in tight formations. They were very loud and Erin covered her ears with her hands as she giggled when they passed overhead. My favorite part was walking into the cargo aircraft I used to work on. I could begin my stories to the kids with, "I load planned and loaded aircraft just like this." That gave them a chance to be properly impressed, but I have to say their favorite part of the show was riding an aircraft simulator that had them spinning upside down. How can these stories compete? Next time I'd bring Popcorn. She always listens to my stories. John Galvin, a freelance writer for "Runners World" magazine, made a visit to this marathon to write a story about the 50 States Club. His very well–written article came out in the June 2005 issue. I was excited to see my name near the very end.

43

The Spooky Story
May 29, 2004

IDAHO

1,686 miles

For this trip we decided to take Popcorn along. As I said before, she's a good listener and never complains that the drive is too long, and this was going to be a *long* drive. Jeanne and I had two weeks off from work together for the second year in a row, so we were going to try to work in three states and three marathons. I was going to drive straight through, 26 hours for the 1,686 miles, according to "Map It." I could do it, right? Wrong! We ended up in the middle of Wyoming in the dark and in pouring rain, and to top that, with road construction such that there was only one lane in each direction. All that's not on the "Map It" plan of travel. They picture a sunny day in June, with four lanes, at least. At 2 a.m., I had suffered enough and pulled into a rest stop to sleep. Naturally, my car companions, who had all been asleep, woke up. "Where are we? Why are we stopping?" The same questions were in Popcorn's bark. She was ready to play if we were going to stop. Trucks rolled by, using their noisy "Jake" brakes. To be sure, I had no sleep. By 3:30 a.m., most of my words comprised four letters. I might as well drive. No sooner was the quiet hum of the moving van going than "Snore." They were all asleep again. Anyone for an airplane? How about a breakfast stop? They all ran in to eat, and I slept in the quiet van. By the time we made it to Boise, 28 hours after we started, they were dashing to the hotel pool, as usual, and after I had my runner's packet, I hit the sack. These tired legs had miles to run the next day.

The Run

Again, despite the almost sleepless drive the night before, I had my goal of breaking four hours. All right, my times had been a little depressing this year. There had been the usual priorities of work and family, family and work. So, I'd be happy with an under four hours rather than a Boston qualifying 3:15.

We were bussed to the start area. It was a crisp and beautiful morning. I loved everything about this place, now that I was finally here. It was a small park along the Boise River. I had a good feeling. Then the gun went off. Bang! My legs started running, but instantly they reminded me I had put them through a 28-hour drive. "Give us a break, already," they whined. Okay, this wasn't going to set any records, but I did complete the first mile in 7:35. However, I knew my legs felt too heavy, and my splits (time per each mile) would diminish quickly. That's exactly what happened. I was slower each mile. By mile 14, I knew it would be another long one. (But wait, aren't they all the same length?) At this point, I decided not to think about my time, just the beauty of the course. I'd try, at least, to have a nonstop run.

Although I was feeling the hurt, I tried to keep my sense of humor by telling spectators that other people were chasing me and asking if anyone knew where the shortcuts were. It was grueling, but the finish line was gratifying, especially when Popcorn licked me on the face while I was lying on the grass. There was only one disappointment. I learned that Dawn Wells, Mary Ann on *Gilligan's Island*, had been there earlier signing autographs at the finish. She was gone when I arrived. That'll teach me to be so slow. Well, autograph or not, it was a nonstopper.

Time: 4:04:35

With the race being over, it was time to play. This state had such beauty, we decided it was ideal for camping. We gathered our gear and headed north toward the Boise National Forest. We drove alongside the same river where I had run. It was so much more relaxing to be passing it in the van with my family. It was better to have the marathon first. It was Memorial Day weekend, and most of the campgrounds were full, but we found one eventually. It was an absolutely perfect evening, as we moved closer to the campfire to avoid the chilly wind. More than the wind was chilly, however, for some reason Erin was in a foul mood. She vented her anger at the world in general, and me in particular, screaming harsh words at me. It was better for her to get her feelings out than spend the rest of the vacation sulking. I regret I was overtired and returned a few harsh words myself, which didn't help. But where else can you go when

you're out in the wilderness by a warm campfire? There are not any doors to slam as one escapes to one's room. She walked around a while and cooled off, and in a couple hours, we were friends again. The term "special needs" child doesn't just apply to education. They need special emotional support even more. I was glad we were all here together. I took out some meat patties and created a flaming show of slightly overcooked hamburgers with a few mosquitoes per burger for flavor. Usually I throw in some moths and gnats, but none were available. (At home I let Jeanne cook, as when I was a teenager, I cooked over the campfire).

That night under the Ponderosa pines was even more beautiful than the evening had been. There was enough space between the trees to see the Big Dipper and even a few satellites zipping by. In the morning, after fair eggs and horrible pancakes made with a crummy mix, we headed for Erin's favorite, horseback riding. For that we went to Gary Towne's Stables, where the guide, Gary, of course, decided we should climb the mountain behind his house. Climb a mountain on a horse? Was this guy nuts? Didn't he know my fondness for heights? Well, it was Erin's special treat, so I gulped and followed along on the zigzag path. As luck would have it, my horse and Erin's were in a constant feud, and Austin's horse kept stopping to eat grass. I wanted to get to the top and back down, with no pauses for eating anything.

Gary, being the experienced guide that he was, saw the horses were feuding. He tied up his horse and led Erin's horse with all of us in a line behind, me in the back. That system worked, and I started to actually enjoy the trip a slight bit, taking a look around. Gary answered all of Erin's redundant questions and gave a running speech of his own. He showed us the bluebells, Wyoming's state flower, the smell of the ponderosa pine, kind of like vanilla, and a spot where a weather balloon had fallen. He also pointed out an eagle's nest on the absolutely highest branch of a pine, away from everything and everyone. Peaceful, but probably boring. On the trip down, I was relieved to see, was an old logger's road that ran along the same stream where we were camping. I asked Gary if there was really gold in the stream. "Well, a couple of prospectors come out once or twice a year with a machine, and they always find some specks. Once in a while they find a nugget or two." That didn't sound sure enough to quit my job and start looking.

We returned safely to the corral, Erin walking her horse at the end because she was sore, but Austin finally gained full control of his horse. Jeanne had a look of, "What can I do?" The horse led her to a water trough at the end of the corral. She needed lessons from Austin, but by then we were all glad to be getting back in the van for a ride on soft seats over which I had control. The van stopped to eat, but only when *I* decided it was time.

After our horseback riding, I decided to continue our western experience with fishing. I had purchased a three–day license, so I hoped I'd be able to catch some trout. We passed an area destroyed by forest fire in 1989. It has been left like a laboratory, to see how long it takes for the plants to grow back naturally. It was sad to see what damage a fire could do, and we knew how important it was to watch our campfires. We kept going until we saw what appeared to be a fishing pond. Stopping, we saw there were already too many fish-ermen, so we drove on. In a few minutes, we were at the bottom of a mountain with a trail leading to the top. Just a short walk, we figured, to find a stream for Popcorn to have a drink. The few minutes turned into a two–hour hike. As Popcorn lapped the water, I saw sparkles in the stream. I pulled out a rock the size of my fist. It actually had a lit-tle speck on it. It looked like gold, all right. I put the speck on my index finger to save it. "Jeanne, look! No more work. No more scrap-ing and saving." "Wow! You're rich!" she laughed. However, a little spec is difficult to hold on to, and it was gone in the wind in less than an hour. Oh, well. We were having fun. Erin hardly complained at all on the climb up, and I told her how proud I was. As we sat by the campfire that night, I realized I already had my gold, all around me. We played our "create a spooky story" game. Each one would say a sentence to add on to the story. Austin and I learned that Jeanne and Erin could not tell a scary story if their lives depended on it. Each time the story went off track, Austin and I would put it back with our additions. We got to one part in the story, "Austin and I were follow-ing a trail in the dark," To which Jeanne added, "There was a grunt-ing noise coming from the other side of the bushes." By then our story was so long and convoluted, I was about to give up, but instead I put in humor. "As I peeked through the bushes, I saw a bear, but he was-n't grunting, he was farting." Then Erin, as if on cue, blurted out,

"Like this!" She lifted her leg and let out a long and thunderous fart. We all rolled in laughter.

On day three, the van took us exactly where we told it, up to Boot Hill in Idaho City. There we saw grave markers dating back to the mid 1800s. There was an effort to refurbish the cemetery, but that would take a <u>grave</u> effort. (For the first time since I began writing this book, I hear, "Boooo!") Some of those buried had come for the gold rush and ended up there. Others were successful and left with their gold. Who knows how their lives were after these discoveries. Gold makes changes, but what kind? Gold was part of history. I had to get back to the present. Tomorrow was a trip to the Oregon run. That night we had another great evening camping, roasting marshmallows and popping corn. The next day, before heading to Oregon, we stopped at the starting point of the Idaho marathon, where I decided to get an eight–mile run in for some conditioning. I don't like running, but I actually enjoyed this shorter run along the river. On our way back, a large group of school kids on bikes came by, and they all admired Popcorn. "What a pretty dog." "Oh, I love that dog!"

I felt proud to hear the comments, but Popcorn was not impressed. She was just happy wherever we went. She enjoyed our first few days in Idaho, and was just as glad to return after our visit to Oregon. (See chapter on Oregon.)

Idaho Again: As soon as we were back in the potato state a week later, we visited Mountain Home. The main attractions there were sand dunes, but I wanted to see more. When I was in Hawaii, I had sent most of the low level toxic waste to Mountain Home. I wanted to see the Envirosafe landfill, where the waste ends up. I called the manager and he gave me permission, as long as the rest of the gang stayed in the van in the security area. "Okay," I agreed, and we started the drive out there, to what is now called U.S. Ecology. At the site I left them in the van, and the manager, Jim, picked me up in his truck and we headed out. In Hawaii, I had heard that there was a large hole in this place with a plastic lining, so that nothing toxic could end up in the water table. As it turned out, there was several feet of barrier that included clay and a poly liner. In addition, below everything there were several basins, sort of like sump holes in your home. If any liquid accumulates, it is pumped back out again. Jim informed me that it was a rare occasion when a pump was run, and it was usually due to moisture. He said the closest water table was 1,800 feet down. What was more interesting, he told me that the site was over an old Titan Missile base, so there was a maze of tunnels below us. He also told me there was waste from the production of steel sent there from other places, and they cleaned the waste of toxins before they placed it in the landfill. I left with an appreciation of all that was done, but then I was ready to get back to regular tourist sights.

We went on to the sand dunes, which were fun to climb on. Then it was time for the state's famous product, potatoes. An hour into the drive, in which I had no plans to stop, Austin said, "Mom, I got to go to the bathroom." I figured he could hold it, so I kept going. Five minutes later he said, "Mom, I've got to go real bad." I'm not sure why he was talking to his mom, since I was the one doing the driving. I passed a sign that indicated the next rest stop to be 69 miles away. Ten minutes later Austin said, "I can't hold it any longer." I replied with, "You have to. There isn't any place for me to pull over. Just think. When I do stop, you'll get to experience one of the greatest feelings ever known to man." After he pleaded a little more, I pulled over to the side, where he quickly got out, ran up the embankment, hunkered down behind some sagebrush that was half his height, and smiled.

Not long after that we made it to the Potato Museum. There, we saw the world's largest potato chip and bought potato–type souvenirs. We learned that only by irrigating was it possible for Idaho to grow those great potatoes. They're thirsty little critters. On our way out of the state to Utah, we saw irrigation systems in place. I'd appreciate those systems when I ate my next baked potato.

44

The Great Fishing Expedition
June 6, 2004

OREGON 2,057 miles

If ever two fishermen tried hard to catch just one little fish, they were
Austin and I in Oregon. We tried from the banks of the lake and
from out in a boat. But before we tried, there was a brief stop as we
crossed into the state. We had to see the Oregon Trail Museum,
where Erin was delighted by the collections of crystals even more
than by the history. Then we drove to look for a camp site. We passed
a few, but they were all too close to highway noise. I'd never get any
sleep in those places. Keep going. There had to be a quiet place in the
state. A few miles up on Route 35, we saw the most spectacular sight
in Oregon, snowcapped, solitary, massive Mount Hood. While still
admiring the breathtaking beauty, I glanced in my rearview mirror
and saw across the river, in Washington, Mount Adams, just as
impressive. It was certainly worth leaving Chicago to carry with us

the memory of such splendor. And it was marathons that motivated us to be out here.

We couldn't just look, we had to stop and rest. With the help of Jeanne's AAA book and a friendly ranger, we ended up by Lost Lake. Even the name suggested we'd find some quiet. It had just that, and we pitched our tent. After that, we followed a path around the lake, declaring it just the place for fishing the next day. Then it was time for a restful night. On schedule, bright and early, Austin and I were up with our worms and down to the banks of the lake. We found the perfect spot that had the most awesome view of snowcapped Mount Hood directly in front of us. The lake acted as a mirror, capturing the reflection of the massive mountain. The fish were jumping around and biting worms, just not ours. Oh, well. We had three nights for Lost Lake. We'd catch some later. We did see some fish, but they were in the fish hatchery we all visited. There were plenty of trout and salmon being raised, a real boon to the local economy. No fish hooks allowed. Maybe a little work before pleasure. Just as I had done when the kids were little in Hawaii, I took out bags for collecting trash around the lake. It was men against women, with a $5 prize for the team that collected the most trash. Erin did a great job, but with the weight of a wet diaper, Austin put us over the top.

Work completed, Austin and I had time for another try at fishing. The fish were not cooperating at all. Okay, we'd go where they congregated. The next morning I rented a rowboat and headed out. We could see that trout were swimming under the boat, so I felt we had a good chance. It was a windy morning, so it was difficult to row to the other side of the lake. Once there, we cast our lines. Nothing. We got out for a snack and asked the store clerk if we were doing anything wrong. He said we had to add marshmallows, so he sold us a bag. We went back out. The wind blew us to shore, and I rowed us back out. It blew us back, and I rowed out again. And again. And again. After two hours, the limit on our boat trip, we had to return. I explained our dilemma to the renter, and he said I should have put down the anchor. "There wasn't an anchor," I insisted.

Back to fishing from the banks. We saw a man 30 feet away catch a trout. Then an old man and two little girls rowed in front of us, and one yelled, "I got one, grandpa!" After that, I saw through my binoculars another family's kid catch a fish. Austin and I: zero. We'd find

another hobby. For now, my hobby was running, and it was time to go for my packet. The packet pick–up was delayed, so we made a trip over the bridge to Washington for the state sign photo we'd missed two years before. Then we paid $12 for a camp site on the Washington side and went to the Hood River Museum. More history, this time by video. The kids now knew more than any of their classmates, I was sure. They didn't just know the history, they could feel it, having been where it happened. They were learning our country inside and out. The video suggested visitors visit the impressive Multnomah Falls. We took its advice. It was cool. We hiked the long way to the top for photos. As always, Popcorn accompanied us, and as was becoming very common now, all along the way we heard, "Great dog. May I pet her?" I could have set up a petting booth and made a fortune. I don't know if Popcorn would have wanted a cut.

Night was approaching, so we went back to the campground. We had plenty of space in our area because everyone else was in RVs. There was even a horseshoe game, where I beat Austin in a few games. Then, before it was dark, it starting pouring rain. Erin and Austin chose to sleep in the van. No complaints. It would have been an understatement to say Jeanne and I had a good time by ourselves in the tent. The noise from the steel bridge traffic didn't bother us at all. We did feel like the first train that rolled by was going to roll right over us, but we got used to the sound. One thing was certain though; no one could hear the noise coming from inside the tent.

The Run

I got everyone up at 4:30 a.m. so we could cross the bridge to where I could catch a bus to the start. This run offered two starts, 6 a.m. and the official competitive start of 7 a.m. I was a 6 o'clock guy all the way. The buses were late, and our driver had no clue where the starting line was, but we finally made it to the start in The Dalles. We actually started at 6:20. Seeing my T–shirt, a lady behind me hollered, "He's a fifty–stater." That was a good start. I held my lead for four miles until another runner caught up with me. We ran together under a cool, overcast sky, passing only a dead rattlesnake. The runner and I kept at the same pace until we reached a hill, where I slowed a little. He passed me and was out of sight before too long. I was on my own, but the scenery was, indeed, as gorgeous as the fliers had promised. Over the next four miles, four other runners passed me, including an Australian lady. I had a tough time on the hill, but the view made up for it. Somewhere around mile 17 or 18, when I started to really rough it, I just thought that this was a case of pure enjoyable scenic misery.

This event also included a half–marathon, out and back, which started and finished at the marathon finish. At my mile 20, they were at their turning point. When I approached 21 miles, I passed the leaders going the other way. A total of five marathoners had passed me, but now I was alone again. It was a neat feeling going one way while half–marathoners were going the other way, cheering me on. They were going up the hill, while I was going down. By mile 23, I was overtaken by several runners. Were they half–marathoners or full marathoners? It didn't really matter. I was only running against my own time. I just wanted to keep it less than four hours. I didn't want to fall apart and blow it. As I approached the end, I saw my little clan and Popcorn waiting. I grabbed her leash and let her run the last 50 feet or so with me. She was very excited and jumped up and down as she ran across the finish with me. With Popcorn's help, I finally broke four hours for the first time this year. What a relief! There was a bonus. Since I was one of the earlier finishers, I was able to get a massage right away. The therapist asked me if I was feeling any kind of abnormal pains. He noticed my pelvis seemed to be off–center. I told him that for the past few weeks I'd been feeling a burning pain on my right side with sensations of no feeling at all in some places. This problem didn't bother me when running, so I thought I'd be able to ignore it until I completed the states.

Time: 3:55:13

There were two more sights I wanted to show them. One was the Nike campus, where shoe designer John Truax gave us a tour. There, he shared some of the history of Nike that began with Coach Bill Bowerman, who brought the idea of jogging to the U.S., and with the help of an accounting student, Phil Knight, brought running shoes from Japan. Eventually, they created their own running shoes, Nikes, which propel the feet of so many runners today, including yours truly. He told us that the word Nike was actually the Greek goddess of victory.

I was impressed by the size of the campus. It was very well manicured. There were running tracks, a large workout facility, a large lap pool and a large rock climbing wall. There were entire buildings named after sports legends like Lance Armstrong, Jerry Rice and Barry Bonds. The best part of our visit was the mini manufacturing facility. Here, designs are made into prototypes and go through rigorous testing. The shoe we witnessed being assembled had over 50 parts to it. Before we left we were all given a gold Nike "Swoosh" that came from leftover material that was used to make Michael Johnson's running shoes for the 2000 Olympics. The second sight I wanted them to see was the magnificent Pacific Ocean. We took Highway 26 to Route 101 and ended up in a small town appropriately named Seaside. I drove right to the beach, where I took a picture of the mighty Pacific Ocean, living up to its name, peaceful. A perfect end to this breathtaking state.

45

The Flyin' Fryin' Pan
June 12, 2004

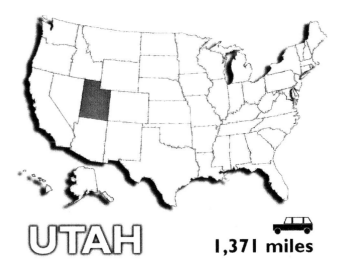

UTAH   1,371 miles

We left Idaho with what we thought was enough time to find a campsite and set up before sunset. It didn't happen. The scenery to Park
City was good, but our time wasn't. By the time we found a site in
the town of Herber in the Wasatch Mountains, we were setting up
camp by the light of the van. It was a good choice, though, near a
small stream with no other people around. The only noise was the
sound of the water rushing by. Perfect.

We slept peacefully, and in the morning were ready to see the
most famous sight, the Great Salt Lake. In the early 1950s, tourists
were swimming all over the lake, held up by the salty water, taking
pictures of each other floating. Now, the smell is like a sewer, or at
least rotten eggs, so there are very few swimmers. In fact, the
marathon literature warned not to go to Salt Lake. We went, but we

didn't swim. We rode on an eight mile long causeway that went to Antelope Island in the middle of the lake. There was a small harbor with six boats anchored. We drove past them to the visitors' center. Inside we learned that the lake is fed by four rivers, but it has no outlet. The water evaporates, so the water that remains is more and more concentrated, as it sits on a deposit of salt. The only life that can stand the salty mixture are tiny brine shrimp. The boats skim the top for eggs that are frozen and sold to hatcheries.

After the center, we braved the smell and went down to the water's edge. We walked about 100 yards into the water before it even reached our knees. The water looked filthy and brown, but it wasn't because of dirt, it was the zillions of shrimp. We cupped our hands and filled them with the water, watching the tiny creatures swim in our hands. Then we had to hit the outdoor showers to remove all the salt that caked our legs.

The water had only this tiny life, but the island had large buffalo. We passed one herd running toward the beach and another herd that could not decide if it wanted to cross the road or not. One buffalo just backed against a tree to scratch himself and stare at us. So we waited until they all made up their minds and crossed. They were truly the rulers of this land. Who argues with a buffalo? From the island, we also watched a sand storm take over Salt Lake City and wandered through a disused farm. The farm was from when the island was private land and a family lived there. They left behind their farm equipment and even their photo album, so tourists could take a small trip back to the 1950s. There was even a tame deer, Whisper, that Austin and Erin got to pet and which Popcorn thought was her

private playmate. But there was no place on the farm for us to cook a meal, so we had to leave it and head to our present–day campground.

Nestled in the middle of the mountains, I got a fire going and began the painstaking art of creating perfect hamburger patties. Erin requested a burger just the right size for her mouth, and I set out to fulfill her request. I patted and pushed until there were seven patties of just the right size. I set these works of art in my pan on prearranged wood over red–hot coals. I knew exactly when to flip them so they would turn out to be masterpieces. I'd pull the pan off the fire, turn the burgers and return it. Then, before I could pull the pan the fifth time, a stick slipped, and they all fell in the fire. With gloved hands, I rescued them, brushed off the ashes and dust, and started again. Finally, they were ready and smelled tasty. I pulled the pan off and pressed down the burgers one last time. Crack. The handle snapped in half, and I watched, in slow motion, my precious products of intense labor turn over and over, landing in dirt. Profanity flew, old words and new ones I was making up. Erin began to laugh. Jeanne, knowing my fuse had reached its end, told Erin to go play. She happily ran down to the stream to tell her brother. Jeanne sat at the table covering her mouth with her hands, trying to keep a look of seriousness as I danced around stomping hamburgers into the ground. I reached down for the frying pan and sent it flying over the mountain. We had hot dogs and marshmallows that night. After that, our meals would be at restaurants. Later on I got in a short run with Popcorn.

However, a short run with Popcorn at this altitude convinced me I was gong to have trouble with this marathon. I was very winded. Perhaps no more training. I'd try more sightseeing. So off we went to Temple Square in Salt Lake City, where we were treated to an impressive organ recital in the Mormon Tabernacle while it poured rain outside. A special moment. The square also displayed a movie about Jesus, as well as many brides and grooms on the way to weddings. With this, we had seen one of the most famous parts of Salt Lake City, but Park City awaited us.

Friday morning, as we packed up to go there, we noticed the mountains around us had fresh white snow, and we remembered that we were going to the home of the 2002 Winter Olympics. Once in Park City, we went to Olympic Park. We toured the ski museum and rode a bobsled. We expected Erin to be upset that she wasn't tall enough to ride one, but she was actually relieved, so away we went. It turned out to be an expensive 68.8–second blast. We had the "three–for–the–price–of–two" discount, so Jeanne rode for free. We had an Olympic hopeful steer the sled, and we had a faster time than the college guys ahead of us, beating them by four–tenths of a second. I guess they got more for their money; they had a longer ride. From there we went up to the ski jump slope. I can't imagine anyone wanting to ski down that. We were ready to get down and scour the city for an expensive spaghetti dinner. Then we relocated to a different campground for the night. It was noisier than the other, but much closer to the starting line. Getting ready for the next day's start, I left the family in the campground and went to the pasta dinner to pick up my packet. I sat at a table with Jack, a marathon walker from Iowa I had met in Oklahoma and seen in Delaware. We listened as the featured speaker was introduced, an 81–year–old lady, and ultramarathoner. After this introduction, the lady at our table, Helen Klein, rose and showed a 22–minute video of NBC's Dateline coverage of a 350 mile eco–challenge she had participated in nine years ago. She spoke of the three Ds for marathoners: Desire, Dedication and Discipline. I thought that if I only had discipline, I could qualify for Boston. I felt honored I had sat next to her and had obtained her autograph. However, the pleasure of sitting at the table with Helen soon evaporated. The race director was at the same table, and seemed to be an agreeable and reasonable gentleman. I wanted to ask him about starting the race early, since I never sleep well beforehand anyway, and we had a very long drive in front of us after the run. According to the literature, others in the past had started early. I just had to make sure the time would be official. Then Helen's husband, 15 years her junior, jumped in with his song and dance about why runners should not be allowed to start early. I wasn't exactly told no, but I was encouraged to follow the schedule. So my next agenda was Popcorn. She had trained with me, and this looked like a good course for a dog. The race director had no problem with the idea, but guess who did? Next time I won't ask questions in front of marathon celebrities.

The Run

So, I was going to make the run without Popcorn and start at the scheduled time. While the kids slept in, Jeanne and I drove six miles to the start. As I left her, I told Jeanne to expect a four–and–a–half–hour finish. I would just stay ahead of Helen, who was also running this marathon. Actually, once the run began, I felt better than I expected. My first three miles were around seven minutes each. Then things changed. We turned around and headed in the opposite direction into a very strong wind, turning my miles into nine minutes each. We were at a gradual uphill going against the wind until about mile 16, and then the hill became really steep. I had time to enjoy the scenery, though I missed Popcorn. (During my more delirious miles, about 20 something, I ran by a man with a very nasty bump on his head. When I asked him about it he told of a crazy story about being in the Wasatch Mountains three nights ago when a frying pan came out of nowhere and hit him in the head!)

Around mile 22, I was passed by a golden retriever and then by a female runner. She said the dog was hers and it had run with her the whole way. It was having a casual trot, while she struggled on. The last couple of miles were tough, but I didn't fall apart. I actually would have broken four hours if it hadn't been for the wind. That was all right. I was happy with the seven minutes over, and delighted with the sight of Popcorn. Jeanne brought her so she could run the last

100 feet with me. She was a sight, jumping up and down with joy. By then my frustrations from being discouraged from starting early and running with Popcorn had dissipated. Although I didn't exactly agree with their reasoning for not having early starts or dogs, I felt it was truly an honor to sit at the same table with Helen Klein and her husband. They are very special people.

Time: 4:07:10

That's the beauty of these marathons. The people are terrific. After a stretch and change of clothes, we headed home. Of the three runs so close together I was able to break four hours on only one, but they were all nonstoppers. Since the Wyoming part of the drive home was in daylight this time, we were able to enjoy the scenery. I made it home in 21 hours. I have only a few more states left, but I knew the next one would be the toughest.

46

Blistering Speed
August 22, 2004

COLORADO 1,070 miles

My family won the bravery award in this state, walking across the Royal Gorge Bridge, the world's tallest suspension bridge, a thousand feet above white water rapids. Whoa! I gulped silently, trying to keep my love of heights to myself, so no one could tell I'd rather be off this bridge and on solid ground. I walked right down the middle to get an equal view of both sides. About halfway across, I felt some rumbling under my feet, and the bridge swayed back and forth. Double gulp! But there I was. I had to stand still and rock with it. Then I saw the cause of the rumbling. There was a car right behind me. Funny, the driver seemed to think he had the right of way. No time to argue. To my chagrin, I had to move to the side and let him pass. I breathed deeply and waited for the rumbling and swaying to pass while the rest of my crew, unfazed, merrily bounced along. Once on the other side,

we were offered all types of activities: helicopter rides, whitewater rafting, horseback riding, fishing, camping, all for a price, of course. We were short on money and time, so we settled for some awesome scenic photos and then eased our way back across the bridge. I had driven fifteen–and–a–half hours before the bridge trip, so I was more than ready to find our campground. Jeanne had picked it two months before because it was close to the marathon site. Proximity to the start was all it had going for it. They gave us a microscopic space between two RVs to put up our five–person tent. The campground was right in the middle of town, so we heard every car that passed. They also charged double the amount of any campground we'd been to. Oh, well. No time to think of amenities. I had a run to focus on. We wandered around, finding our way to the outdoor expo for my packet, ignoring the far off dark clouds and lightning. By the time we were back, everyone was famished and wondering, "Where are we going to eat?" No one mentioned my building a fire and cooking burgers. I wonder why. Okay, I wasn't up to cooking anyway. I collected my tribe and headed to Italy, in the form of an Italian restaurant, for my favorite, spaghetti. While we ate, the rain arrived in full force, with winds driving it sideways. I looked over at Jeanne. "Did you close the window flap on the tent?" I knew the answer I didn't want to hear, a quiet "No."

Well, there was nothing we could do, so we kept eating and even ordered a pizza to go. If I had built a fire, it would have gone out anyway. We just waited, and the sun finally came back. Walking back to the campground, we found six inches of water in the tent. Our blankets were soaked. Time for the driers. Three hours and $10 worth of quarters later, everything was back to normal, and I was ready for sleep. I had only had an hour's nap at a rest stop on the drive, so I had settled in and was snuggled up to Jeanne when I felt my shirt getting wet. What now? It was a bottle of Gatorade minus top, which had tipped over. Was this a sign from God I needed to drink more Gatorade? At last I fell into an off and on again sleep, thinking of that run. It was actually going to be up Pike's Peak! I thought of all the information and warnings that came in the marathon literature. As with all trips, I wanted Austin and Erin to learn something. I thought they'd learn a little history with this mountain. As it turned out, Zebulon Pike was an explorer, but he never set foot on the mountain named after him. No problem. They would remember that Pike's Peak was in Colorado and their dad climbed it; simple geography. For me, I would be getting more than geography; I'd be getting a lesson of the physiological demands climbing that mountain could have on a human being. I had read the marathon literature. It warned that if runners thought they could take on Pike's Peak without extensive training, they'd be sorely surprised. Six months ago when I had read this, I intended to train harder for the run than ever before. Did I follow through? No way. Nothing in my life changed to accommodate extra training. I had worked more hours so we could pay for these trips, even working 81 hours in one seven–day period. As the race date approached, I had become more and more nervous. In the two weeks before the run, I had done a nine–miler and a five–miler. That was it.

The literature had emphasized another factor over which I had no control. It told us that the altitude would affect each person differently, but there was no denying that those who lived and trained at higher elevations would have, in most cases, an advantage because their bodies would have produced more red blood cells. It went on to tell us that exercise physiologists had determined that, for the general population, it would take about 10 to 14 days for the body to begin adapting to lower levels of oxygen in the air. I didn't have 10 to 14 days. I had 25.5 hours to adapt to being at 7,000 feet. Then, in the description of the ascent, we were advised that the course was a relentless uphill grind. There were no downhill sections to permit recovery. Combine that with the continued drop in oxygen as the elevation increased the physiological demands would be exceptional. Great. The most uphill training I had endured was running up the stair truck to access the 747 freighters at work. In addition, they stated that most of the trail was narrow, so passing was difficult or impossible. Thanks. With all this on my mind, you can see why my eyes were wide open before the rising sun.

The Run

I did not feel well already when I arrived at the start, and I would have just as soon not have been there. I did a couple of warm–up jogs and found the literature was right. I was out of breath. I mingled with the other runners and heard things like, "I'd be happy with 7.5 or 8 hours." Eight hours? I could not fathom taking that long for a marathon. I had an initial goal of breaking five hours. That was before I had studied the literature so well. Now I was setting my goal at six hours, despite my lack of enough training. While I was waiting for the starting gun, the announcer informed us, "There will be storms and lightning around noon on the summit, so try to be on your way down by then." I was confident. Naïve maybe, but confident. It was 7 a.m. then. I would certainly be on my way down by 10:30. No problem. Precisely at 7 we were on our way. I stayed toward the back to get my wind for the run. Surprisingly enough, catching my wind was not the first difficulty. Five minutes into the run, my calves became tight. They stayed that way most of the first hour. Despite this, during the first 1.3 miles, I ran at a casual pace, even passing a few runners. As soon as we hit the trail, it was another story. We were no longer in a run, but in a swift walk toward the summit. At this point, there was no way to pass even if I were to hike faster than those in front of me, so I just went with the flow. Along the way were signs telling us how much farther to the top. These signs seemed to take forever to reach. It was frustrating because I had to

just stay behind the long line of people in front of me. We were all in
this together, like a long tail. Well, I was in excellent scenery, and I
was conquering Pike's Peak, so I finally relaxed a little and enjoyed the
trip. There were even spots to step out of line to enjoy the view or
take photos. For myself, I knew that the higher I went, the less I
wanted to look out. I kept going. I remembered that the literature
had also stated that the trail was often narrow and winding, with
gravel, rocks and dirt, as well as sharp turns and abrupt changes in
altitude or direction, but there were no exposed ledges, so there was
no danger in falling off. Bullshit! Even with my oxygen deprived
brain, I could sense plenty of places to fall off the trail. I say "sense"
because at four miles from the summit and higher, I could only look
straight down at my feet, not over to the sides. About three miles
from the summit, I began to personally understand what John
Denver meant by "Rocky Mountain High." I was feeling it. If I
looked up and out, I'd get wild sensations of dizziness. I was only
okay keeping my head down, looking at the trail. At this point, I saw
feet facing the other direction. The leaders were on their way back
down. Those of us on the way up had to stop and lean a little to let
them by. With a little less than a mile to the summit, I came upon
another runner who looked in bad shape. He said he was okay, but he
didn't look it. I walked with him for a half mile until I was sure he
could make it to the top. We let a whole bunch of runners pass us, but
I didn't feel comfortable leaving him. A few feet before the summit, I
was greeted by Jeanne. She had brought Popcorn, Austin and Erin up
the easy way, by car. Actually, it wasn't that easy a trip. The road was
steep, too, and she had to have her brakes checked on the way back
down. Well, I was glad they were there. The kids were playing around
in the grass, but Popcorn bounced up, excited to see me, giving me a
doggie smooch. It was good to take a break.

It had taken me a depressing 4 hours and 37 minutes to reach the
top. I remembered, however, that the literature said the ascent takes
most runners the same time as a normal level marathon plus thirty
minutes. In that case, I *was* making good time. It usually took me 4
hours to finish a "gut it out" run. As I left to go down, I told Jeanne
to expect me to make it to the finish in about three more hours. That
would make it a seven–and–a–half–hour marathon. I never would
have thought it possible, but then I hadn't seen Pike's Peak before.

Now I had to face the trip down, which was another concern. The trail was treacherous. One could easily stumble and get hurt. I saw some pretty nasty scrapes on other runners. I wasn't thinking so much of time any more. I just wanted to get down safely. This was really like two runs. In other marathons, I thought about how many miles to the finish one mile at a time. In this one, I thought of how far to the summit and then how far to the finish. Going down, I felt energized. My only focus was not to tumble. The first five miles down were actually fun. Despite the obstacles, I was moving at a swift pace. Then, when I was at the marker for 7.9 more miles, I felt like I had stones in my shoes. I kept going because usually stones work their way to an open area in the toe of a shoe and don't bother me so much. These didn't. They stayed in the heel. I had to stop. I took off my shoes and shook them. Nothing. I put them back on, and it felt worse. I took off my socks. Nothing. I put everything back on and tried to just go on my tiptoes or walk. I was feeling a burning sensation on my heels. I examined them and found blisters. I hadn't had these on my heels before. Well, keep going, Marlin.

Then I saw a runner take a tumble in front of me. I stopped to help him up and stayed with him as he hobbled along. Finally he said he was fine, and off I went, as well as I could go on blisters. It got worse. By 5.9 miles left, the blister on my right foot ripped open. I was on a mountain trail where there was not going to be a car passing to take me to the finish. Nothing to do but continue forward, gingerly. I walked and stopped, walked and stopped. Another runner came by with a bum knee. I gave him an extra knee strap I had, and he thanked me and trotted away. The guy with the twisted ankle also passed by me. I just kept on my slow pace of walking, stopping and running a little on my toes. "Ouch" was not strong enough a word. My foot burned unbelievably. I knew the skin on my left foot was going to break soon, too. Then I looked at my watch and realized at this pace I wouldn't even break eight hours. Psychologically, I didn't want to face that. I knew if I could run nine–minute miles, I would be under eight hours. Did I say run? I could barely walk, but run I did. I made some "err, uugghh" noise along the way from the excruciating pain. I grimaced through the final stretch and, two steps past the finish, I collapsed in a chair.

As I was taking off my socks, several volunteers came over to ask me if I was okay. "Sure, except for my feet." When they saw my feet, their expressions were full of pain, too. A doctor and a nurse were brought over to attend to me. As the doctor pulled out his scissors to cut some skin he warned me, "You're probably not going to like me right now." I figured there was nothing he could do that would

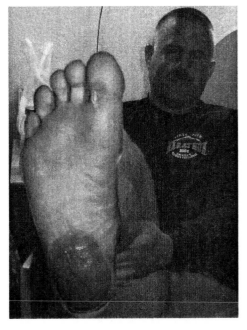

make the pain worse. I was wrong. He did make me feel a little better, honoring me with the skin award of the day. There had been many blisters that day, but mine were the worst so far. There were 211 runners who came in after me. I hope none of them had the agony of beating my painful blister record. I'll never know. I just knew my feet were going to get some tender care before I took them to North Dakota.

Time: 7:58:14

This marathon was dedicated to my dear friend Father Pat, who passed on July 22nd

47

Losing By a Leash
November 11, 2004

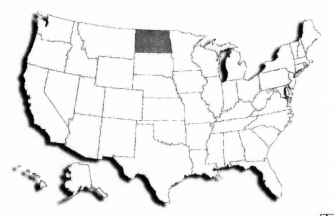

NORTH DAKOTA 827 miles

Would you believe it? In less than a month those feet were healed, and we were heading west for another marathon. This would be our last one to the west. We would kind of miss that, because we enjoyed riding in the uncongested open spaces, through lands we'd never been through before, modern day Lewis's and Clarks, with a few extra comforts. Even when we slept under the stars, we had a map and usually knew where we were.

We took advantage of those comforts, stopping for the night in Minnesota to enjoy a good night's rest and meals. After breakfast we headed toward North Dakota. On the way to Bismarck, we were going to catch a glimpse of the world's tallest structure, a television tower. However, there were no signs indicating where the tower was, except we knew it was a little north of Fargo. We did find two very tall ones, but we couldn't figure out which was the tallest. So we sent Austin up to the top with a measuring tape. Not! Instead we took pictures, so whichever was tallest; we have a photo of that one. Further on, we stopped so Popcorn could study the map in the visitors' center, and to pose with the world's most humongous buffalo, at least 24 feet high. (I have a feeling he's not real. He stood very still for the photo.)

We found a buffalo–free campsite, where they guaranteed no rainstorms to soak our blankets this time. Then we went for my packet, and I was delighted to hear that Popcorn could run with me. On the way back, we stopped at Fort Abraham Lincoln, where Custer and his men slept before their battle at Little Bighorn. We were guided by a costumed guide through the house where Custer lived and through the soldiers' barracks. Each bunk bed had the name and history of the soldier who slept there. What a sad end to the lives of young soldiers and young Native Americans before they'd had much chance for life.

On a lighter note, we were treated to a visit to the hens, where Erin was given an egg to take with her back to the campground, but

I still wasn't doing any cooking. I stopped on the way home for dinner to make sure of that. Then it was time for a decent night's sleep. We were by the peaceful Missouri River. Perfect, I thought. That was before midnight. That's when the noise began. There were a couple of hours of high–pitched, skin crawling yelling. I was startled at first, but soon recognized it from when I had camped as a kid. An owl. A stupid screech owl was in the tree right above us. I don't know how Austin and Erin slept through the racket, but Jeanne and I lay on our backs with our eyes wide open staring straight up. Another pre–run night with very little sleep.

The Run

The star of the run, of course, was Popcorn. Before we started running in the cool drizzle, she greeted her fans. Then the gun went off, and she was ready to run. She didn't like people in front of her and passed quite a few, but not enough for her taste. I took a more casual pace because I already knew I wouldn't break four hours. I was just proud to be running in my Continental Airlines sleeveless running shirt. Because of my blisters from Pike's Peak, I had not run an inch since then, and my legs felt very heavy. Popcorn gave me the encouragement I needed, as she trotted quickly along, enjoying the friendly comments from the few spectators. At the halfway point, we stopped for Jeanne and the kids to give "Jeanne's dog" some water. After that, they met us every three miles. I was glad I had brought Popcorn along, but at about mile 22, she was limping a little. She didn't seem to want to stop, though. I raced her to the finish and she barely won by a leash. I checked her feet and found several burrs. She hadn't wanted to stop despite these—a true marathoner.

Time: 4:25:28

After a shower and lunch, we went on to the awards ceremony. I really like this part. It's always nicer to be sitting down watching people smile than running. Now for a ceremony with a little difference, a Native American powwow, or conference, celebration, get–together, fiesta all in one. At this powwow we were going to see competitions in song and dance. It was being held at the packed United Tribes Technical College. We could hear the sound of chants and drums beating as we tied Popcorn to a tree and walked toward to the grounds. Once there, we saw it was like a county fair. Vendors were selling jewelry, blankets, shirts and food, including frybread, which looked like puffed up tortillas. We made our way through the crowds in the stadium to four empty seats on the top row. Luckily, we sat next to Connie, a Native American who was very knowledge-able in the dance traditions and customs. She had been a dancer herself, so she explained the message of each dance. There were dances related to war, rain or a lost spirit. She explained what the chants were about. Also, she told us that this powwow was the final one of the year, with the winning elites competing. I was impressed

by the skill of the men and women, but even more so by that of the kids. They obviously took the activity seriously, and this showed in their dances. At one point, the spectators were invited to join in a dance, and Erin and I accepted the invita-tion, moving in the circle to the rhythm of the drums, a great feeling. Erin was even allowed to pose with the Miss Indian Nations Pageant winner. Then Austin was down there for photos, too. Afterward we tried the food, which was delicious. A perfect ending to another great marathon trip.

48

Nifty Fifty
November 14, 2004

RHODE ISLAND 983 miles

This trip began with a drive without Jeanne. She had to work, so she had to fly straight to Providence. Austin, Erin, Popcorn and I headed east in the van early Friday morning. We could not pass up a little detour to Bellefonte, Pennsylvania, to visit Mary Ellen and Popcorn's mother. Popcorn was six months old when we got her, and I was curious to see if she would remember anything of her old home. Other than wagging her tail at other dogs that looked like her, she didn't seem to recognize anything. We thanked Mary Ellen again for Popcorn and told her how much we all loved the dog. Then it was on to Scranton to visit Uncle Raymond's and Aunt Judy's farm. We arrived just in time to help feed the calves. I always like the kids to have a taste of what I experienced as a child. Just a taste was enough. One of the calves had its chain snagged. Right away we freed the calf, but it already was bleeding from pulling so hard to free itself. Sizing up the situation, Uncle Raymond reached for a bunch of cobwebs from the ceiling and laid them on the wound. I didn't say a word, but I thought there was no way cobwebs were going to help. To my amazement, when I checked the calf in the morning, the wound had closed and the calf was ready to eat. I guess farmers have been doing that for years, but we all learned something new to us. Actually, I learned later cobwebs were once used on humans, too. The best part of the visit was a big farm breakfast, with conversation and the warmth of family.

We headed out and soon were in the Providence, Rhode Island, Airport in time to meet Jeanne. For the past four years, during November, we had been fortunate with the weather on marathon trips. Rhode Island welcomed us with snow on the ground and cold, but at least it was sunny. Since the state was so big, it took us an entire afternoon to see half of it. We didn't have time for the other half, as our hotel in Coventry was waiting. Over the past few years, the Ocean State Marathon was the only marathon in Rhode Island. The organizers decided that because of limited participation and difficult logistics, they would just hold a half–marathon in the future. How were those of us in the 50 States Club going to complete our 50? Fortunately, not far from Providence, in the town of Coventry, there was a run called the Nifty Fifty. They had a 50–mile run and a 50K run. Those guys were nuts. There was no way I was going to run either of those. Luckily, they added to it a little marathon–size run just for the 50–staters. Thanks. Nifty Fifty took on a special meaning to me in another way. Since I had run four times in Hawaii and I had run in Washington, D.C., this was actually my 50th run! When I finished, I was pleased to receive a medal that read "Nifty Fifty Finisher."

The Run

It began with snow everywhere. I was fortunate to be able to start early and keep my own time. We had a long drive back, and I wanted to get the running part of the day over with as soon as possible. Since Pike's Peak and the sore feet in August, I had run only one other time, which was the marathon in North Dakota. To say I was a little out of shape would be an understatement. It seemed for all of my runs in 2004 I was like that. One other runner started early with me. He was none other than the marathon legend, Don Lang, who was completing his 50 states for the fourth time. I was humbled being near him, but also I felt I was just a little smarter than he was. I was only going to do this once. Anyway, here I was, getting close to my own goal, and, prepared or not, I started down the scenic course, cheered on by no one. Finally, a little past the halfway point, my happy crew slowly cruised by in the van, cheering me on. It was a bit of a comical moment, too. If ever an animal had an expression on her face, it was Popcorn as she stuck her head out the window and seemed to say, "Why are you running without me?" Then she had that begging look that I read as, "Please, oh, please let me run with you." I would have taken her out to run if it were not for the snow. We pretty much had to stay right on the road because the snow was too deep on the sides.

As in my other "gut it out" runs, my legs were heavy early on. By mile 20, the lactic acid had built up so much I stopped and walked a short distance. About a fourth of a mile from the end, I passed a snowman in someone's yard, and had Jeanne take a photo of me next to it. It was a least a foot taller than I am, and must have taken someone a long time to create. Finally, after what seemed like a very long 4 hours, 40 minutes and 9 seconds, I crossed the finish line. I had felt every minute of it, but at least I was across.

Time: 4:40:09

We made the drive back special by stopping to see my grandmother. The only other time Austin and Erin had seen her was when we went to my mother's memorial. My grandmother's beloved partner of 40–plus years, Tex, had passed away in October. Tex had been a unique character who resembled one of the Hatfields. He suffered from Parkinson's, and I remembered as a youngster watching his hand shake as he lit his pipe or when he aimed a gun at a groundhog. I never did understand how he could shake so much and still hit his target. Since I hadn't called in advance, Grandma was really surprised by our arrival. The lady has had a tough existence in her 80–something years. Her house on a hillside above South Edmeston, New York, is run down and needs repairs. As I approached her hill, I hoped I would find her well. She had always seemed to be out–of–sorts and grouchy. Then I thought that, just as I wanted Austin and Erin to know I had once been young, I should remember Grandma had been young, too. I tried to picture her as a little girl, running and laughing in those hills with a baby doll. Had she once played ring around the rosy or hide and seek with friends? Or had the work and the worries of life made her bitter at an early age? And what about my mother? Had living with sourness and struggling to survive made her leave home too early forcing maturity to soon? I had always tried to break this cycle by passing laughter and love to our kids. For now, I was glad to see Grandma because she is, and always will be, family. She came out yelling for us to stop screaming at her cat, also named Popcorn, as we hollered at our Popcorn, who was chasing her chickens. Despite that beginning, she was very glad to see us. She actually was pleasant to us all. We told her we'd be back the next morning to take her to breakfast, but we didn't get far. The van had a flat. Austin and I tackled the job of changing it. I was reminded of the movie "A Christmas Story," although Austin didn't lose lug nuts or say "Aaww fuuudege." We finally were able to get the tire on and take off, but we were back the next morning to take Grandma to breakfast and out to the cemetery where Tex is buried. We took photos and promised to send her copies. That didn't happen because the computer crashed, and all photos of the Rhode Island trip were lost. Well, at least we have the memories. No computer can take them away.

Now it was time to figure out what I was going to do for Massachusetts. How could I run there when I didn't have a qualifying time?

49

Run For Research
April 18, 2005

MASSACHUSETTS 1,014 miles

At the end of 2004, I had four states left for marathons and visits. Jeanne and I mapped out our plans for three of them: Maine, Vermont and New York. Massachusetts was still in question. Believe it or not, this state does have marathons besides the one in Boston. There was going to be one on February 27th right outside of Boston. Since I never reached the qualifying time of 3:15 for my age group to run in *the* Boston Marathon itself, I had to contemplate running in that other marathon. What choice did I have? During this adventure, my training habits had never changed. I knew I could have run a 3:15 marathon if I had been able to put in the required training. But instead of improving, my times had diminished because I wasn't putting my heart into the training needed for that elusive goal. I had always believed I was going to qualify, so I wasn't prepared to deal with the reality of approaching the end having still not done so. This dilemma tugged on my mind for quite some time. What could I do? I wanted to run the Boston Marathon, not a neighboring one, so I needed to find some way to qualify. In January, before signing up for the February 27th run, I decided to seek out an alternative way of being accepted in Boston. I knew that certain charities sponsored non-qualified runners for predetermined charitable donations. I also knew that finding a slot within a charity this close to the run would be very difficult, if not impossible. As expected, when I researched the various charities over the 'net, I found that all of them had closed their applications. Instead of giving up, I decided to email some of them just in case something opened up. As luck would have it, Tom Gearty, manager of the Run For Research Charity supporting the American Liver Foundation, responded by advising me there was one slot left. I could take it if I had my application and fee to him in one day. My run to the post office was faster than any marathon I had run thus far. The next day I received his confirmation that I was in; fabulous news. I was finally going to run *the* famous Boston marathon. This is the oldest of all the U.S. marathons; the first one was on Patriot's Day in 1897. The city itself is over 300 years old with some of the original buildings still there. I was going to be part of thousands of runners in this special run. Kind of exciting for someone who doesn't like to run, but is out there anyway, plugging away. It is good to be part of something so positive.

Our trip began at midnight Friday night as soon as I was off work. We made the drive to Boston in 14 hours and 20 minutes, which gave us plenty of time to get ready for a 6 p.m. dinner engagement with the Run For Research team. The dinner was a well organized, class act. We were informed, as well as entertained, by the various speakers. We were deeply touched by some of their stories.

Jeanne actually had tears listening to a fellow runner tell the audience that he was running for his dad who was fighting liver cancer. I, too, was moved by what I was hearing. Before this dinner, I had only looked at the charity as a means of getting a number to get into Boston. In my mind, I felt more shame than anything else for not qualifying. However, as I sat at my table and listened to stories of the lives affected by liver cancer, I began to understand that just maybe I wasn't supposed to qualify by my speed. I was supposed to be there on that night and learn about a disease that has affected more than 25 million Americans. I also learned of a vital organ and the critical role it plays to keep me healthy. I was witnessing this small team of individuals that was absolutely dedicated in its mission to increase awareness of this deadly disease and fight to prevent and cure it. As the evening progressed, my feelings of shame for not qualifying shifted to feelings of shame for not taking my responsibility to this charity seriously enough. At the end of the evening, there was an awards ceremony for the largest contributors and others who made substantial impacts on the cause. One concern I have always had with giving to a charity is where the money goes. As I watched the awards given out, I realized they carried more sentimental value than anything else because the awards handed out were dollar–store types. That was a good indicator that the donations received by the ALF were being put to good use. By the end of the night, I was very proud to be a member of their Run For Research Team.

Sunday was a perfectly gorgeous day for us to tour Boston. We walked everywhere, enjoying the city and the sights. We relaxed in the park at the Boston Commons. We walked through several 17th and 18th century cemeteries that were right smack in the middle of the city between large skyscrapers. One of the cemeteries was the resting place for Paul Revere. A short distance from there was his preserved home, right next to a very large modern building. History and the present are friends together in this city. At his home, we were treated to a monologue by a lady portraying his second wife. She made us feel that we were really there in the past. After her talk, we toured Paul Revere's home. We had hoped to get in a Red Sox game, but we had brought our dog Popcorn. She saved us from overspending. The perfect weather and the marathon weekend made the sidewalks a little crowded. Press from around the world was there. As everywhere we have traveled with Popcorn, she was the main attraction. Jeanne and I must have stated over a hundred times, "Yes, she is a Bernese mountain dog." And just as many times we heard, "May I pet her?" She loved every bit of it.

At the end of the day, while we were walking back to our van a couple of miles away, I experienced a twinge in my left knee. I knew right then I had a problem. Instantly I was afraid I might not be able to run. I became moody and irritable as I limped the rest of the way to the parking garage. I could only envision how many people I would let down if I didn't run.

Back at the hotel, I lay in bed while the rest of the crew went out to eat. My knee began to swell. Even worse, I did not have my miracle knee straps I had used in the past. It was Sunday evening, and all of the sports stores were closed. I knew I would not be able to run very far without some kind of support on my knee. I waited to tell the family the news.

However, on the way back from dinner, Jeanne had stopped at a pharmacy and purchased a knee brace. When I looked at it, I instantly thought, "This isn't going to work." It was too big, and it would rub my leg raw. I didn't have a choice. I had to give it a try.

The Run

The Boston Marathon is always held on Monday, Patriots' Day, which is a state holiday. Because it is *the* Boston Marathon, the oldest, most famous and most publicized marathon in the country, it didn't start until noon in order to have more television viewers. The only good thing about that was I didn't have to worry about sleeping in and missing it. I could think of nothing else that was good about a marathon starting late, especially on that day. A runner's worst enemy is the heat, and it was sunny and 70 degrees. This was perfect weather for the spectators, however, and there were over a million of them.

Our hotel was five miles from the start in Hopkinton, and Jeanne had to drop me off nearly two miles away because of closed roads. I quickly found a couple of other runners to walk with to the starting area. I was curious to know why they did not have their numbers on. I learned they were locals who ran every year. They told me that the race officials overlooked those runners, allowing them to participate in this city's traditional race. Knowing that this run had a cut off of 20,000 registered runners, I wondered, with this new information, just exactly how many people were actually running?

The start area was packed. Each runner was assigned a corral based on his/her number. I was number 16,944. That meant my starting point was behind nearly 17,000 other runners, almost a half mile away from the starting line. I was there an hour early, and while

I waited, the hot sun began to cook my exposed skin. Although I was wearing the knee brace, I was very worried about not making it. I was also wearing my bright orange Run For Research singlet. This made it easy for the runners of my team to identify one another, so we could give each other encouragement. While waiting, I heard over a loud speaker the start of the elite women, which began 20 minutes early. Then the wheelchair race began, there was the national anthem, a couple of fighter jets flew overhead, and then the gun to start went off. Yes, the Boston Marathon had finally begun. Okay, so why was I just standing there not moving? Oh, I remember. I had to wait for 16,000–plus others to start moving first. Four minutes later, I took my first step forward, and then stopped. A few seconds later, I got in two steps and then stopped again. A couple of minutes later, it was stop, go, stop, go. After 17 minutes and 20 seconds, I reached the actual start line. Yahoo! The first mile was a nice downhill. On both sides of the road, there were spectators cheering for the runners. Let me rephrase that. There were *thousands* of spectators on both sides of the road cheering the runners on. This was truly a neat experience. Here I was, finally running the Boston Marathon.

What I did not know was that my progress was being followed by my friends at work. I had a microchip on my shoe, and my time was recorded every five kilometers along the course. Anyone with a computer and a participant's number could follow a runner. A poster was put up, and each time I crossed a timing mat, my time was added to the poster. I felt some minor discomfort with my left knee, but overall the brace seemed to be working and not chafing my leg. The huge number of spectators actually made this run fun. I was able to keep a pace of just over eight minutes a mile. This wasn't going to be any record run for me, but besides just finishing, I had two other goals. I wanted to break four hours, and I wanted to run nonstop. I would be a happy man if I could just do that.

There were a couple of places on this course other than the downhill's that inspired me to run a little faster. The first such place was near mile 12. As I was running, I began to hear a distant, high–pitched hum. The further I ran, the louder it became. I knew I was closing in on some kind of commotion. It wasn't long before I could see the source of this high–pitched, high decibel noise. I was

running past Wellesley College, an all–girls school. For about a hundred yards or more, there were women lined up along this fence on
my right several bodies deep, screaming at the runners. Some were
holding signs saying "Kiss me." Others read, "Give me a hug." Many
were leaning over the fence allowing a view of what nature blessed
them with. Without question, this was my favorite part of the Boston
Marathon. What I do question is, "Why did I choose to run faster at
that point instead of slowing down to absorb the scenery?" As I
moved on by Wellesley College, the high–pitched music gradually
faded away until it was gone altogether.

The second euphoric portion of the run came past the 16th mile
mark. There, a group of Run For Research supporters blew whistles
and cheered me on. I was feeling very proud of wearing my orange
shirt and running for a cause. That was not the only place on the
course where there were supporters of the ALF. Throughout the
entire course I received hundreds of "Go, Liver" cheers as I ran
toward Boston.

Mile 20 brought on Heartbreak Hill. It slowed me down just a
little, but it was no Pike's Peak, and it did *not* break my heart. I got
up and over it and was able to maintain a nine–minute–mile pace for
the final five–and–a–half miles. As I got closer and closer to the finish, the crowds became larger and larger. The cheering crowds motivated me to pick up my pace during the final mile. When I did, I
experienced cramps in my calves, so I slowed back down to my regular pace. Finally, after 4 hours, 15 minutes and 41 seconds from the
starting gun, I crossed the finish line. Since it took me over 17 minutes to get to the start line, I did the actual 26.2 miles in 3 hours, 57
minutes and 53 seconds. I broke four hours and ran it nonstop.
Yahoo! Besides a good speed, I had raised more than $2500.00 for the
American Liver Foundation. And all of us, the Run for Research runners together, raised over $1 million, I learned. That was even better
than the time.

Time: 3:57:53

The bad part about the finish line was that it was overcrowded.
No Jeanne, no kids and no Popcorn waiting for me at the end. It took
me another 30 minutes to get to our designated Run For Research

team meeting place at a nearby hotel. After a terrific massage from a specialist brought in by the team, I was ready to go. The problem was that this city wasn't ready to let us go. It took nearly two hours to get from the parking garage to our hotel, 20 miles away. I guess no one knew that we had a 15–hour drive in front of us.

When all was said and done, Boston turned out to be a wonderfully unique experience for me. As with some of our other destinations, more time would have led to an even better experience for everyone else. Even if I were to qualify someday, I don't think I would want to do that run again. It's just too crowded. Then again, thinking about Wellesley College, I just might change my mind.

50

Lobster Anyone?
May 15, 2005

MAINE
1,145 miles

Arriving in the cool coastal town of Portland, Maine by regional jet Saturday afternoon, we rented a car and made the two–hour–plus drive up to Kingfield, a quaint mountain village where the marathon ended. This little place looked like it really belonged in the Old West with its clapboard stores and old–fashioned hotel. The run was a point to point one, all on Route 27. We rented a condo near the halfway point at the base of the famous ski resort, Sugarloaf. During the drive, we could see the marathon mile markers on the road. Instead of going directly to our condo, we decided to continue traveling on Route 27 to see what the entire course was like.

Near the 10–mile mark, we saw two vehicles pulled over on the right side and people out looking across the highway. As I slowly drove by, Jeanne and I could see they were looking at a moose standing, almost camouflaged, between some trees across the road. I continued on, thinking about the literature I had read that stated we were sure to see many moose in this area. Surely we'd have plenty more opportunities to see some before we left. Right then, I was more interested in seeing what the hill at mile eight looked like.

On our return, we witnessed the same people on the side of the road, but this time with their cameras out. Jeanne and I saw the moose in the same place, but Austin and Erin missed it. Again, I chose not to stop in favor of just getting our long day of travel over with and checking into our condo. We never saw another moose the rest of our stay in Maine.

The Run

At least I would get this run out of the way prior to our two days of being tourists. In the 28 days since Boston, my training had consisted of two nine–mile runs and one six–miler. I wondered if that would be good enough for me to achieve my goal of under four hours.

As usual, I had trouble sleeping the night before. There was an early start for walkers at 6 a.m. Then the regular marathon began at 7 a.m. Because I couldn't sleep, I decided to go for the 6 a.m. start. Also, since Boston, my left knee had really been bothering me, and I wasn't even sure if I could make the whole distance. About 10 of us started early in the cold clammy rain. This was like California all over again; I was in first place. The rain was coming down hard, and a small stream developed in the middle of the road.

When I had reached the one–mile mark, the first of four buses carrying runners to the start passed me. Its wheels were perfectly aligned with that stream in the center of the road, and as it passed me, I became the recipient of a huge splash the size of a large wave. It was just like what you would see on television. As I approached mile two, I saw a grey fox with something in its mouth run out of the woods and up the embankment to the side of the road. When it saw me, it dropped what it had and turned around and quickly disappeared back into the woods. When I was over the spot it had stood, I looked down to see a headless rabbit. I could only hope that it came back for its breakfast after I was much farther down the road.

I managed to do okay the first seven miles, but the hill at mile eight kicked my butt and reinforced the fact that I did not enjoy doing this. I did like the course, at least, because it was in rural back country. However, there was way more traffic than I expected. The noise of the vehicles passing took the serenity out of the run and kept me from really appreciating my surroundings. A little before mile 20, the leader overtook me. Two minutes later, the 2nd place guy passed me. They were running like it was nothing as I struggled to continue on. Remember, I had a whole hour head start on these guys. It was not long after that I was passed by several other runners. Finally, after another nonstop run in the rain that seemed brutal to every inch of my body, in 3 hours, 57 minutes and 6 seconds, I crossed the finish line.

Time: 3:57:06

But wait. No Jeanne and no Austin or Erin. I was a little frustrated not to see them. About five minutes later Jeanne pulled into a nearby parking lot. It turned out that about five of the runners had decided it was their privilege to run right smack down the center of the road, not allowing any vehicles to pass. Because of those inconsiderate few, it took Jeanne nearly an hour to drive just 12 miles. For the most part, I feel my fellow running community is made up of the most wonderful people you would ever meet. However, as in almost any other group in society, there are the rogue characters who live by an expectation that the rest of the world should adapt to their individual whims. Every so often, as a supervisor, I have to deal with similar circumstances at work. I've concluded that it is people like that who make the rest of us look good.

After a massage, some stretching, a few photos and checking us out of our condo, I drove my crew east to Bar Harbor. We stopped at a nice mom and pop restaurant along the way for lunch. I was hoping we would see some moose, but no such luck. All we saw was rain and more rain.

Bar Harbor is a fishing village on a small island in the Atlantic Ocean called Mount Desert Island. It was a rainy, chilly, gloomy afternoon when we arrived. This made the shelter of our hotel room seem inviting. We did a little touring of the downtown area, passing an 1800s hotel in the drizzling rain before calling it a night.

On Monday morning, we booked ourselves in for a "Lobster and Seal" boat ride. The weather was still drizzly and cold, so there were only two other people who went for the ride. This turned out to be an absolutely excellent experience for all of us. Our naturalist, Sasha, did a wonderful job of explaining the details of the lobster industry. As we went out, we noticed hundreds of different colored buoys in the water. Underneath each one there was a lobster trap. A few miles out our captain pulled alongside a buoy, which he knew was his because of the color coding, and he proceeded to pull up the trap. The trap had a bunch of rock crabs in it, but no lobsters. Each trap he pulled had crabs in it. On the seventh pull, we finally had a large lobster. It was pulled out of the trap, and Sasha, after banding the claws, went on to explain all kinds of neat stuff about lobster. We learned they can be either right or left–clawed and how to differentiate between male and female. We also learned size limitations for keeping one or returning it. We all got to handle the lobster. Erin acted as if it were a cat and held it close to her face for a picture.

During this boat ride, we also passed a nearby island and watched a bunch of seals hanging out. There was also a lighthouse on the same island. In addition to giving us a chance to handle the lobster, the boat also contained a touch tank with several specimens of underwater life that we also were allowed to handle. Included were a starfish, a sea cucumber, a spider crab, a snail, a sea urchin and two more lobsters. It was so nice that on a boat that could have held 50, we were the only ones. It gave us a chance to spend extra time asking questions and holding the sea life. This was especially a treat for Austin and Erin. During this two–hour excursion, we also witnessed porpoises and dolphins swimming alongside our boat. They were almost close enough to touch. The dolphins seemed as glad to see us as we were to see them.

After our entertaining boat ride, we headed south back to Portland. Before checking into our hotel near the airport, we drove an extra 40 miles further south to get a shot of the state sign. Once we were back at the hotel and checked in, we decided to go to Portland's waterfront for dinner. We chose lobster at a floating restaurant from where we could see the water, cruise ships, fishing boats and oil rigs. It was also where the final bill matched what we had paid at the Seattle Space Needle, but you don't eat fresh lobster right out of the ocean every day, so we ordered and enjoyed our feast. However, I informed all my crew that the same rules applied as at the Space Needle; no one was allowed to use the bathroom for a week.

Back home on Wednesday, Jeanne and I had an IEP meeting with the group of specialists involved in Erin's modified learning program. This had been a tough year for her in school. Back in November, we took her out of her mainstream school and moved her into a modified learning program at a different school. At first, this was traumatic and difficult for her, but in the mainstream, she just kept going backwards, and it was like dealing with Austin all over again. She qualified for special help because she had the Turner Syndrome label. The problem was that Turner Syndrome was more of a physical issue than a learning disability. After Austin had been diagnosed with Asperger's, and we read Tony Atwood's book, Jeanne and I knew Erin had Asperger's, too. All of the characteristics were there. We had mentioned this at two previous school meetings without getting any acknowledgement or agreement. They told us there was no need to get her a separate diagnosis because she already had a label. "Okay, that's fine," I said, "but we need to deal with her needs based on what we know, regardless of whether or not she has been given the label 'Asperger's'."

The school didn't see it that way. They left her mainstreamed until it came to a point where something had to be done. Now at this meeting, which included Erin's new teacher, Mrs. Dillon, who was instrumental in turning Austin around, we received our desired response. This group, especially Mrs. Dillon, agreed that we were, indeed, dealing with an Asperger's child. We sighed with relief that someone had finally agreed with our diagnosis. At last the powers in charge of her school education saw what we had already seen. We knew from being her lifetime teachers.

The result was that Erin's junior high curriculum will now be based on the unofficial label of Asperger's Syndrome. Prior to Austin's diagnosis, we referred to that time when we didn't know why he acted as he did, as the "dark side." Although AS was first described in 1944 by Austrian physician Hans Asperger, it was only very recently that teachers and psychologists have begun to recognize it and address it. Parents everywhere had been in the world of the unknown, along with us. With Erin, we had been on the dark side as well. Now, finally, we were back in the light with both of our kids. It doesn't really give us a road map of what their futures could be, but it gives us a feeling with Erin that we've been there before, and we can handle it. We have a book and the internet to give some clues, but we know from experience what works.

An emotionally gratifying moment at this meeting was Mrs. Dillon explaining to the group how much a normally quiet Erin talked about her trip to Maine and the lobsters. We already knew the value these trips were having on our kids, but it felt especially good when the teachers reinforced that fact and added that the spillover effect was good for all of the students in the class. Just hearing her say that made us beam, and I was happier than I've ever been to be taking them on these marathon trips. Now we look forward to two more to complete the set.

51

Granite Art
May 29, 2005

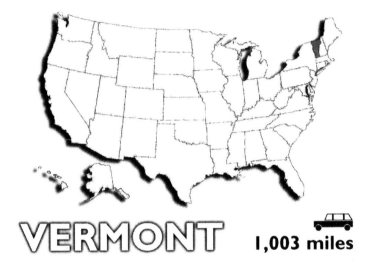

VERMONT   **1,003 miles**

For the third year in a row, Jeanne and I took two weeks of vacation at the same time and we pulled the kids out of school a week before their summer break began. In the previous two years, I had managed three state runs in each of those two–week vacations. This time I was looking at just two more, and then the madness would be over. Yahoo! But before I could get too excited, I had to repeat some of the more undesired necessities to make this happen. That is, I had to work my regular 10–hour shift Friday evening, and then drive 16 hours to Burlington, Vermont. Even though I ate M&Ms and drank Red Bulls along the way, I believe my thought processes were what kept me the most alert.

Of course, shortly after we started the drive, everyone else, even Popcorn, was sound asleep. Austin was to my right in the navigator's seat, with his knees nearly touching his chin. That kid had grown so much since we started this adventure. Now those long legs made him look uncomfortable, since there was no longer enough room for him to completely extend them. Erin was sitting directly behind me. I could see through the mirror that she had headphones on, and I could barely hear her CD music. Her head leaned on a pillow propped up to the window; her mouth was wide open. I could almost distinguish the Zs coming out of her mouth. To her right was my best friend in the whole world, Jeanne, leaning on another pillow, sound asleep. Then there was Popcorn, lying on the floor between Austin and me, occasionally lifting her head to receive a light pat that acknowledged her presence. It was my goal to put as many miles behind us as possible while they all slept.

We arrived at our hotel at Essex Junction, Vermont, just a little after 4 p.m. Saturday. I was whipped, but it was good to know I had 16 hours to rest and relax before the run. On second thought, I don't think I have ever experienced relaxation the day before a run.

The Run

Sunday morning came quickly. I found myself in sight of Lake Champlain in Burlington, ready to start an hour early. The streets were full of waving well–wishers on sidewalks lined with bright green maple trees, or sitting in rockers on their porches. While I waited, a lady walked nearby with a Bernese Mountain Dog. Naturally, I had to go over and pet it and tell her I had one, too.

It wasn't long after that the runners were all bunched up eager for the start. Clouds threatened rain, but they also made it cool enough to make the morning pleasant. Once I began to run, I was again reminded that this wasn't a pleasant activity I was doing. My legs were heavy and tight right from the get–go. I tried to ignore what I didn't like and focused on the idea that when this was over, I would only have one more left. Now that was a pleasant thought.

The course took us through the city and out to the country and looped back through the city again. This was good, because it allowed me to see my crew four different times. During the run, I saw three more Bernese Mountain Dogs along the course. So when I passed Jeanne, I told her there were three more Popcorns out there. She smiled, but I knew she thought there is only one real Popcorn.

Somewhere a little past mile nine, I noticed my legs seemed to loosen up. I actually felt comfortable for the next seven or eight miles. I realized a sub four–hour finish was achievable if I didn't fall apart during the back half. Around mile 17, I developed a side stitch that I couldn't shake off for the next four miles. I had a nonstopper going, so I wasn't going to upset that. I kept running on. By mile 20, one of my legs was feeling the burn; I noticed I was slowing down. Fortunately, I had already banked up some extra time and could afford to be slower. Eventually, my side stitch went away, and I worked my way through those last miles. It was, indeed, a pleasant feeling to be greeted at the finish by my crew. Even better was the thought that now I was down to 26.2 miles left.

Time: 3:55:12

After the marathon, I did a Superman–style clothes change at a nearby mall. Then we walked around Burlington. We found it to be a thoroughly enjoyable little city in the middle of two mountain ranges. We watched two men using chainsaws to make ice sculptures out of blocks of ice. As we admired their work, a man passed with another Bernese. Of course, this dog and Popcorn had to get to know each other, which we gave her time to do. Then we went on exploring, ending later for dinner at a restaurant by the shore of Lake Champlain. We ate outside and watched the ferry boats cross back and forth from the New York side. Looking across the lake, I couldn't help but think that it was only 50 miles into those mountains that in two weeks I would finish this adventure.

All the time the sky kept threatening. We brought our camping gear with hopes of spending a couple of days in the mountains, but the weatherman kept calling for rain. So instead, we spent one more night in our hotel.

The next day we decided to make the trip we missed in April, a visit to Cape Cod. On our way across Vermont, we stopped at a granite quarry called Rock of Ages. We were treated to a narrated tour where we learned of the time–consuming extraction process. We also learned of the history and value of granite as well as its current uses. The most notable is for memorials in cemeteries. We were told of a couple of nearby cemeteries where there were some very artistically carved headstones. We went and saw the guides had been right. There were all kinds of granite headstones in a variety of designs. One was carved as a race car, another as an airplane. There was also a soccer ball, a cube and two that were like beds. There were so many fascinating designs; it was as if we were in a museum instead of a cemetery.

Once we were back on the road, the rain came down hard. By the time we made it to Cape Cod that evening, it had stopped. Again we chose a hotel over camping out. It was sort of comical because we located the hotel we wanted to stay in and then made a reservation over the phone across the street. A minute later we showed up and checked in. We picked up some tourist fliers in the lobby and went to our room to figure out what we were going to do. Our time constraints allowed two nights and one full day. We chose the whale watch cruise.

The next morning we were at the harbor to catch our boat. It was an excursion advertised as three–and–one–half hours long with a guarantee to see whales. It was a cold, windy and fog–filled morning. Our boat was large and had inside and outside seating areas. It could hold over 200 passengers, but I figured there were around seventy on this trip. So it wasn't overly crowded. As it left the harbor, we couldn't see very far because of the fog. Once out in the ocean, the visibility was a little better, but we saw no whales. After what seemed an eternity, especially for cold Austin and Erin, a whale was spotted. Our boat turned, heading to the area of the sighting. The captain stopped the boat and we drifted for a while. All of a sudden, everyone rushed to the other side of the boat. A large whale had surfaced right next to our boat. Excited tourists were exclaiming; "I see it," "It's so big!"

I was able to get one good picture. Then the whale went to hide from his admirers underwater, and that was it for the day. At least we saw one, but overall it was a disappointing trip. I guess Jeanne and I were spoiled by the boat ride we once took in Hawaii from Maui to Molokai. Whales were breaching all around us on that trip. We had expected the same thing here, but it didn't happen. Austin and Erin saw their whale, though.

So instead of being completely disappointed, Austin decided to use a little of his humor to liven things up. Our return was very windy and most of the passengers stayed in the covered cabin area that had large windows from which to look out at the ocean. Austin went on the deck by the window and acted as if the wind were blowing him away. It was so funny watching him that Erin and I had to go do it, too.

Later that day we drove to the very end of Cape Cod just to say we did it. The weather wasn't cooperating very much, so we spent minimal time walking around before heading back. There was a monument nearby memorializing the Pilgrims that would have been neat to visit, but we arrived just a little too late to go in. They had just closed for the day. That completed our Vermont leg. I was ready to wrap things up in my home state of New York.

52

Wrapping It Up
June 12, 2005

900 miles

We departed Cape Cod on Wednesday morning, June 1st, and headed for the Big Apple. It was a gorgeous day, and our drive was relatively short compared to what we were accustomed to. Of course,
when we were in city traffic, our final ten miles took nearly an hour.
The first stop was an animal hospital, where we boarded Popcorn for
two days. With all of the activities we had planned, there was no way
we would be able to keep her with us.

    Our next stop was our hotel, The Hilton, Times Square. I'm real-
ly not sure what we were thinking when we reserved this hotel. It was
very elegant, but it exceeded our budget significantly. As we entered
our fancy room with a view of Times Square, I found myself trying
to calculate all of the overtime hours I would need to work when we
returned home to pay off our maxed–out credit card. Knowing that

this was our final marathon trip helped ease the pain somewhat. A visit to the big city wasn't going to be cheap, but cost wasn't going to stop us from seeing and experiencing what this great place had to offer. So, armed with a little cash and, more importantly, a credit card in hand, we began our tour. The first stop, right next to the hotel, was a wax museum. There we posed for photos next to assorted famous people, including presidents and stars. The likenesses of these figures were impressive. Their eyes seemed to penetrate as if they were real, and on several occasions I found myself looking away from them. After the wax museum, we walked a few blocks to the Empire State Building. We had already purchased our tickets online to save time when we arrived. Once there, we were advised to come back another time because visibility was zero. That didn't seem right in my mind because we had been admiring the height of the building on our walk there. I didn't remember seeing any clouds. I told Jeanne to wait next to the line of people while I ran back outside to assess the weather. When I looked up, I could see the top. There were a few clouds near-by, but they didn't look too imposing, so I ran back in and said we wanted to go up. Many other people had taken the advice and chose to try their luck on another day. This made it a little less crowded. When we reached the top, guess what? It *was* cloudy and visibility was about a quarter mile, like they warned us. So what? We couldn't see that far, but what we did see was enough to give us an apprecia-tion of how tall the building was and of how busy the city under us was as tiny people rushed around in toy cars below. Before leaving the building, we went on a virtual reality ride called NYSKYRIDE. We sat in seats on a moving platform and watched a movie screen that left us feeling as if we were touring New York City in a helicopter. When it was over, we all left with smiles because it was a fun little ride and more than made up for a few clouds outside. When we had entered the Empire State Building, it was light outside. By the time we made our exit, nighttime had arrived. We decided to go back to Times Square and check out the nightlife for a while. I couldn't quite remember the best way to get back, so I pulled out my map to get my bearings. I hadn't looked at it 30 seconds when a man dressed in a business suit walked over to us and asked what we were looking for. We simply told him Times Square, and he pointed us in the right direction. At this point, Jeanne and I began to compare this visit with the one we had made in 1987. That was the first time either of us had been to New York City. Back then, the very first thing we witnessed when we got to the street from the bus terminal was a robbery. When we toured the city on that day, we felt very intimidated, as if we weren't supposed to be there. Things were so different on this trip as a family. We didn't have the feeling of being threatened, and the atmosphere was much more inviting. There were two more times during our short stay that a friendly gentleman would send us in the right direction.

Times Square is an impressive place to visit. There are giant plasma screens everywhere, keeping the people updated on the latest headlines and showing different TV programs and advertisements. We easily could have stayed all night. Austin and Erin wanted to. They were animated by the crowds and lights more than on other trips, and I would have liked to have given them more time, but we had a full agenda of sights for the next morning. Thursday morning we hailed a taxi that took us to Battery Park, where we took the first boat to the Statue of Liberty. At this point in my life there were two things I really wanted to do: run a marathon in my home state of New York and visit the Statue of Liberty. In a few hours, the list would be narrowed down to one. I really can't say or describe what Jeanne, Austin and Erin were feeling. For me, I love my country and all it stands for, and I especially take pride in Lady Liberty and what she symbolizes, not only for our great nation, but also for the world. I thought of the people arriving by boat, thrilled to finally see the welcoming Lady. With my feet finally on Liberty Island, I felt an unbelievably powerful sense of honor just being there.

The security to go to the statue was justifiably impressive. It was considerably more stringent than in our airports. Once past security, we were able to tour the pedestal on which she stands. Today it's like a small museum. There we learned a great deal of her history and construction.

It was interesting to learn she is made out of copper, and the oxidation of the copper is why she is a greenish color. The top of the pedestal was as high as we were allowed to go. This was somewhat disappointing, knowing that in the past people could go to the crown and, in her very early days, even her torch could be visited. I did overhear an employee telling another tourist that one of her perks when she was first hired was a one–time–only visit to the crown. If only I could have convinced them to let us up as I did at Crazy Horse, I would really have something extra cool to write about. However, there were too many people there to even consider trying. Besides, I was thoroughly satisfied by the experience we were already having. Once back at Battery Park, we decided to walk the six miles back to our hotel. On the way, we stopped at the site of the World Trade Center. There was a tall fence surrounding the site, and on it were posters containing the history of the buildings with pictures sequencing the events that took place. Standing in this place, I couldn't help but feel a great sense of sorrow over what had happened. It was interesting discussing this place with Austin and Erin. Erin did not remember what had happened, although she was eight at the time. She didn't seem to comprehend how tragic it was, even with all the pictures. Austin, on the other hand, remembered very well and showed a sense of appreciation to be there.

We took Broadway the rest of the way back to Times Square. The weather was perfect for a long walk. Of course, Erin didn't think so. Jeanne, Austin and I were all looking around at the hustle and bustle of this busy city. There were so many sights, it made the walk seem easy for us, but not for Erin. She didn't care how impressive the skyscrapers all around us were or what the thousands of people were doing. She just walked along staring at the sidewalk. At first she was fascinated by the glittering specks in the concrete, but after awhile this became boring for her, and she began to complain. As much as we encouraged her to look around, she chose to keep looking down as she walked, complaining the entire way. This is part of her personality, so we had to just accept it and enjoy what we were seeing. I was sorry she couldn't see it as I did. Then, as much as I was enjoying the walk, I began to develop my own problem. My knees were bothering me as they had in Boston. I was actually having trouble walking. We slowed a little, but we eventually made it back to our hotel to rest.

Later that evening we went to see a Broadway play. I had chosen "Chitty Chitty Bang Bang," and it turned out to be very entertaining. It was actually a perfect play for both kids and adults. Austin gave it a great review, confiding later that the play was his favorite part of the entire trip. Afterward, we again went back to Times Square before calling it a night.

On Friday morning, I wanted to do one more thing before moving on. If I was going to break four hours on my last marathon, I needed to get in some training. I figured I could get up early, pick up Popcorn and go run the 6.2 miles around Central Park. It sounded like a perfect ending to a great stay at NYC. I had run Central Park twice before. The first time was the most memorable. It was September 11th, 2002, and no one wanted to fly. On September 10th, my friend Weldon and I had decided we were going to take advantage of the open airplane seats. On a last–minute whim, we caught a morning flight to Newark, took the train to the city, walked to Central Park and then ran around it. On the way back to the train station, we stopped at a popular restaurant called Stage Deli, where we were served huge corned beef sandwiches with dill pickles on the side. Weldon inhaled his sandwich; it was gone in no time. I'm a slow eater, so I barely had half mine eaten when we left. We were tight on time, so we had to dash to the train station. It was tough trying to run past thousands of people while eating my sandwich at the same time. We just made our train. One minute later, we would have missed it and missed our flight back to Chicago. By the time we were on our flight, my sandwich was consumed and I was full. The sad part was that the flight going back was emptier than the one coming out, so we were put in first class. Now I'm here to tell you that Continental Airlines serves some pretty darned good meals in first class. But on this flight, I was so stuffed that I had to tell the flight attendant that I didn't want anything. I was quite disappointed over this, but not near as much as Weldon was. Our sandwiches were expensive, and he had paid for them. As much as I wanted to run Central Park again, I found sleeping in a bit more enjoyable this morning. We took our time getting ready for our departure. While waiting what seemed like an eternity for our valet to bring back our van, we watched iron workers assembling another skyscraper across the street. Now that I think about it, maybe that valet didn't take long enough, as our attention had been captivated by the progress of these workers.

After a quick stop to pick up our four–legged friend, we again spent considerable time navigating our way through the city. This time it was on our way out. After a couple of wrong turns, one that put us at Yankee Stadium, we finally made our way out of the congestion and onto the highway. Our next destination was Springville, Pennsylvania, to spend a night at Uncle Raymond's and Aunt Judy's before heading to upstate New York. A visit to their farm is never uneventful, and this short stop was no exception. They have a small pony that the kids were fond of and had enjoyed petting back on our visit of October of 2003. This time the pony had been loose so long that it would not allow anyone to get near it. Judy shared with us stories of when they had several people running around trying to catch it. For nearly a year, that pony refused to be caught. That was until Austin and Erin came along. They simply wanted to pet the pony. So they kept following it all over the fields. When they walked, the pony walked; when they ran, the pony ran. The rest of us watched and laughed, thinking there was no way those kids were going to catch that pony. However, their closeness to animals was, once again, in bloom. Although Erin finally gave up, without realizing it, she had made a big contribution in the effort to capture the pony. Austin kept at it, although it was evident he was getting tired. Jeanne bet him 20 bucks he couldn't catch it. About two hours after the chase started, Austin made a sprint toward the pony. The pony just looked at him as if to say, "I give up!" The pony was more whipped than Austin and stopped for him. Austin, with a grin from ear to ear, put his hands up in victory and quickly reminded his mom she was out $20. Somehow she managed to get that money from my wallet and not her purse. Smooth.

Later that evening, Austin and I helped Raymond with the chores. I asked Austin if he would be interested in working on this farm for a couple of weeks over the summer. To my surprise, he answered full of enthusiasm with hands waving high in the air, "I'd be honored to work here." With that, we made the arrangements, and Austin came back and spent three weeks on the farm that summer. Without books telling us what to do, we had discovered the natural place for them to take small steps toward being adults some day.

Before leaving the following morning, we were entertained by a mother and father robin feeding their babies. They had built their nest right under a rafter on the porch deck. There were four babies, and the parents were regularly bringing worms in to feed them. Erin said it looked like the babies were trying to eat their mom and dad.

Again, it was a relatively short two–and–a–half–hour drive before we were in upstate New York. Our first stop was in the town of Oneonta, where I assumed my Grandma Kay still resided in a rest home. Kay was my stepfather's mother, and she had had a stroke over 25 years before that left her partially paralyzed and unable to speak. We had made a visit in 1999 after the Virginia Beach marathon, and I also came to see her in the spring of 2000 after my own mother passed. Each year we sent her a Christmas card. None of our cards were ever returned, so it came as a shock when we were told that Kay had passed three years earlier. For a long time it had always bothered me that her son, my stepfather, had been buried over 1,000 miles away in Kentucky. This was also the first time I felt as if I could do something about it, if that's what Kay wanted. I'm sure I could still find out, but it wouldn't have the same effect as if Kay were with us. So, with heavy hearts, we headed to Hartwick, 20 miles away, and made a stop at the cemetery where my dad was buried. This was my first visit since my mom's ashes were placed in the ground over my dad's remains. Several plots away there was a memorial stone identifying Kay's final resting place. We had been to numerous cemeteries during our travels, but this particular stop on this day seemed to draw the most inquisitive mortality questions from Austin and Erin. I only wish I had the right answers for them. Does anyone ever?

We spent the next three days in this area where I had grown up visiting family and friends. We had planned on making a nearby state park as our base, but on our first night, we found ourselves conversing at my Aunt Sherri's well after dark. Sherri insisted we stay at her place, since she had rooms available. Austin and I pitched the tent and camped in the back yard, while Jeanne and Erin stayed in the house. Sherri was a great hostess, and we ended up using her place as our base camp during our stay. The following morning we went to Cooperstown to visit the Baseball Hall of Fame. Since Erin doesn't like baseball, she and I stayed outside with Popcorn while Jeanne and Austin did the tour. This saved us a few needed dollars. After the Hall of Fame, we drove over to the farm I had grown up on. Different people were living there this time, and no real farming was being accomplished. There was only a desire to do some kind of farming, yet the owner wasn't sure exactly what. We walked around, and I shared childhood stories about growing up there. Although there was a tragic ending at this place, I am always grateful for the efforts Mom and Dad put into our farm. Memories of my childhood life in this home were precious, and I will forever cherish them. Someday, I know I will have a hand in seeing this place realize its true potential again.

Later that afternoon, it was time for a little redemption for Austin and me. My Uncle Dave, Sherri's husband and my mom's only brother, took us fishing. Austin was a pessimist of the worst kind. He insisted we weren't going to catch anything. I knew differently. Dave is a backwoodsman, if ever there was one. He's a hunter, fisherman and survivalist. He's an accomplished Boy Scout troop leader. He knows his stuff, and he knows where and how to catch fish. So while Jeanne and Erin stayed at Sherri's to do the laundry, Dave, Austin and I went fishing. As we were rowing out onto the pond, we witnessed a baby bird struggling to swim and fly across the pond to the shore. Its worried parent was chirping away, flying around in circles, encouraging it to cross. After lots of noise and considerable effort, it made it. I thought of how I want to do the same with Austin and Erin. I can't run life's challenges for them, but Jeanne and I can be beside them, encouraging them on, as we have on these marathon trips. There were three of us in that boat with six fishing poles. I'm not exactly

sure how he managed it, but Dave had all of the poles going at once. Of course, I was in control of mine and Austin his, but it was still a busy little operation going on. We were out maybe five minutes when Austin caught the first fish. It was a nice–size perch. In the 90 minutes of fishing, we each caught about ten fish. Of those, we threw 20 back and kept ten. We watched Dave clean and filet them before we went back to Sherri's. Our camp out that afternoon was great. We ate freshly caught fish, venison, macaroni salad, chips, and, later, some smores. The best part was reliving the excitement of Austin finally catching a fish on his own.

During our stay we fit in three visits with my Grandma McLean. Just as we did this past November, we prepared ourselves to deal with an angry, bitter person. Since Tex's passing, many people have stopped in to help her. Unfortunately, she has a tendency to snap at them and say mean things. This, in turn, is cause for fewer visits. Everyone really cares about her, but no one wants to deal with the verbal abuse. We were very fortunate during each of our visits. She grumbled about a lot of other people, but she was very nice to us. We took her to breakfast two times. On our last visit, I thought it would be neat to have the kids experience getting eggs from the hen house. The day before, Grandma promised she would leave the eggs for the kids. When we went into the chicken coup, I pointed out where to look. Unfortunately, the smell in that coup was so overpowering that Erin instantly began to gag. Austin grabbed his eggs as quickly as possible and ran out. Both had lost their appetites and were not able to eat breakfast that morning. The smell in Grandma's house wasn't as overpowering as that of the chicken coup, but it was there, and one had to limit the time before an exit to fresh air was required. In the kindest way, I tried to explain this to Austin and Erin, rationalizing what caused Grandma to reach this state of horrendous living conditions. I hope that this experience will have a direct impact on their own personal hygiene as they  go through life. After an early breakfast and some family conversation, it was time to pull camp and relocate. This time it was a two–day base camp at Delta Lake State Park near Utica, New York. From there, we made visits to two of my dad's brothers, Glenn and Walt. After breakfast at Glenn's, we stopped in at the Long Distance Running Hall of Fame on Genesee Street in Utica. I was curious to see if the visitors' sign–in book was still there. When the Hall of Fame opened up six years ago, there was no book, so Jeanne and I went out and bought one. Our names were the first written in it. It was a thrill to see the book and see that it was nearly full.

Before heading to Walt's, we stopped at the Herkimer Diamond Mine. There we spent an hour hammering rocks trying to get to a Herkimer diamond that has 18 facets. If we found any, we would be allowed to keep them, but no luck. We left with only the experience of trying and a couple of rocks to hammer on when we got home. It was fun going to Walt's because this would be the first time for Joyce and him to see the dog they helped me scheme to get. Shannon and Kaylyn were up from Kansas for a summer break, and we all had a good time sitting in lawn chairs in the yard on a perfectly gorgeous afternoon, socializing. Walt cooked chicken on the grill, Shannon made the potatoes, and Jeanne and Joyce put the salad together. Popcorn was tied to a tree just out of our reach. She whined and barked on occasion to remind us she was there. This was a good time with a good exchange of family stories. But not all was good. Walt informed us that my dad's oldest brother, Paul, was fighting cancer for the third time, and his prognosis wasn't very good. Paul was an author who had written several books and was currently working on a book about the history of the Mohawk River. He had hoped to have it completed before he passed on. Unfortunately, that did not happen as Paul passed a few weeks after our visit. It saddens me deeply that we were not able to see him. We didn't get to see my dad's sister Valaine, either, but we were told she and her husband Don were doing well.

Back at Delta Lake, there were plenty of places for me to run. My next, and last, marathon was closing in quickly, and I needed to get some cardiovascular circulation going if I wanted to break four hours. I told myself that I would go for a short run in the morning before we pulled camp and headed for Lake Placid. Morning came quickly enough, and do you think I got up to run? No way! I probably haven't mentioned it yet, but I don't like running, and I had thought of something more important to do. It was 6 a.m., and I got Austin up and told him to come with me. We got in the van and drove off to another area at the lake that had several large empty parking lots. I got out of the van and went to the passenger side door, opened it and told him to slide over because he was going to drive. For the next 30 minutes he drove all over those parking lots, practicing forward and reverse and using the mirrors and signal lights. His top speed was 25. This was not a natural thing for him and, as I had suspected all along, he will require a great deal of practice before taking on the highway. I'm not sure I'm ready for that, but it gave him such pride to start. In the larger picture, the hour was better spent than running. My time would be whatever it was going to be, but the smile on his face when I said, "Slide over, you're going to drive," was a milestone better than any marathon PR. It was time to head to Lake Placid. It was another short two-and-a-half-hour drive from Utica to our campsite at the Whispering Pines Campground, ten miles east of Lake Placid. After setting up camp, we proceeded to drive the marathon course. It was nice and scenic and hilly. I tried thinking optimistically by convincing myself that I still had three more days to train for those hills. Yeah, right. Who was I kidding? I was in for a rough one. Later on we walked to downtown Lake Placid. The highlights of that walk were the two Bernese Mountain Dogs at the Ben & Jerry's ice cream store. The manager owned them and always kept them tied to a bench outside so people walking by could pet them. Popcorn and these two dogs were all excited to be together. Erin seemed more excited than the rest of us, as she kept trying to hug all of the dogs at the same time. We had to keep telling her to settle down, as she has a tendency to overdo everything.

Lake Placid is the home of the 1932 and 1980 Winter Olympics. It is a beautiful and clean place to visit. There were lots of motorcycles as well as non–motorized bikes. Most of the bikers were part of a triathlon training camp. These athletes would be running the upcoming marathon in addition to riding 100–plus miles the day before. If ever I were to entertain doing a triathlon (Am I really thinking such a thing?), this would be the place to train. The roads are wide enough for bikes, and it's simply a gorgeous place to be. From Lake Placid, we went up to where the view was supposed to be spectacular, the top of nearby Whiteface Mountain. Actually, that day the mountain was in the clouds, so visibility was zero. That didn't bother me a bit. I'm sure the view would have been grand had we been able to go on a clear day. We also went to the Olympic ice skating arena, where we read about the athletes who once competed there. This was also the place of the famous United States versus USSR hockey match where the U.S. won the gold. Outside was the track that Eric Heiden had won his speed skating medals on. I would cross the finish line on that same track if I expected to receive a medal for running the Lake Placid marathon. On our second afternoon, we had hoped to have a nice campfire to roast hot dogs and marshmallows over. I had the fire pit ready with small wood when it began to rain. Fifteen minutes later it stopped. Then it started again. Then it stopped. Then it started again. After about 90 minutes of this indecisiveness, we decided to leave the wet firewood, pack up and go get a room. We found an inexpensive hostel to stay in a few miles closer to Lake Placid. Our place was more like a house than a hotel. It turned out to be a better place to get ready to run on marathon morning anyway.

The Run

Race day finally arrived on Sunday, June 12th. The morning greeted us with an unseasonably high temperature of nearly 80 degrees. Fortunately, there was cloud cover to cool things off. I just hoped the clouds would stay around through the run. My name was announced several times over the PA system, along with Don Langs.

Of course, again, I was humbled to be in his presence. This was his 397th marathon. He was 70 years old, and had no plans on stopping. His advice to me was to make plans for future goals, like the Canadian provinces, the continents and reaching the 100 marathon mark. He said if I didn't make these plans, then more than likely I would get depressed. I didn't have the heart to tell him that running more marathons was not on my list of things to do in life. It was fun being with other runners waiting for this run to start. It was being part of a giant special club. Even if I never run again, I knew I would always be part of this group. There were spectators taking my picture and other runners congratulating me. Jeanne, Austin, Erin and Popcorn were all there watching, too. With all the excitement and friendly well–wishers, I became pumped up and confident that I would have a good run, no matter how hilly or hot it was. My strategy during the entire course was to think about what I was going to do and say at the finish line. If I could focus on that finish, then I would do all right. At 8 a.m. the marathon began; a good, exciting start. My thoughts were in check as I ran down the street with the other runners. After about a quarter mile, I was winded, and my legs were tight. My thoughts immediately reverted back to, "Okay, let's just get this mile out of the way." There was a nice steep downhill on the second mile that made things a little easier. After that, it was rolling ups and downs for the next 11 miles until right before the halfway point. There I would have to run up a steep incline and around the skate track and then back down the hill and around the loop I had just run. It took me 1 hour, 54 minutes to get through the first half. I knew the second half was going to be rough. At this point, the only thing I could think of was getting to each mile one at a time. I wanted to think about the finish, but my mind just wouldn't let me. Awhile back, I had rehearsed some things I would say at the finish. I wanted to fine tune those thoughts during the run, but it was as if I had Alzheimer's. My mind was blank. One nice thing about this run was the support I received along the course from other runners and spectators. I had number 50, and they knew this was my 50th state. What I didn't like were the deer flies buzzing around my head along the course. I was flapping my arms and hands in the air trying to catch them. I killed four of them. When I passed slower runners or walkers, I could see those pests swarming all over their heads.

It seemed to take forever to get to mile 25. I really wanted to enjoy this mile near the end of my last marathon after all those years, but those lousy race directors put a nasty hill at the very end of the course. I had the lactic acid burn going on, and that hill was down-right mean to climb. Once at the top, I had to run three–quarters of the track to the finish. Jeanne was waiting at the top and was ready to hand Popcorn off to me, so I could finish with her. My mind had other thoughts going on, and I completely missed the hand off. As I passed Jeanne, I told her I had a stone in my shoe. The local televi-sion station was there to cover my finish. I picked up speed going around the track as Austin ran backwards in front of me as if it were an easy thing. He was such a tall, almost–man at this finish, and he had been just a little fellow when I started. And there was Erin cheer-ing for me, now a seasoned traveler, who had been a shy toddler when I began. And behind them, Jeanne, who had given me encourage-ment these 11 years. We were here. We had made it! I pumped my fists in the air in victory as I crossed the finish line. Then I headed for the nearest chair that I could find. Within a minute, Jeanne, Erin, Popcorn, Austin and the television crew were at my side. Jeanne looked at me and said, "You have a stone in your shoe?" I was really in pain from the lactic acid burn and just nodded my head in the affirmative. She asked if I needed her to take the shoe off. Again I nodded my head. As she looked down to pull off my shoe, I pointed to the TV camera lady to make sure the camera was taping Jeanne, not me. When Jeanne pulled my shoe off, a diamond wedding ring and an engagement ring fell to the ground. She picked them up and looked at me, her face turning beet red. I was completely at a loss for words because I had forgotten everything I had rehearsed. The only thing I could think to say was, "She's my best friend." I felt so awk-ward as I realized that I should have remembered more to say in this very special moment for my wife. As it was, we were both a little embarrassed. Maybe words weren't needed; she knew. But the reporter wanted questions answered as they turned cameras on us. I tried to say something, all the while trying to disguise the awful burn I felt in my legs. I told of the loss of her diamond several years back and my inability to afford another one. I explained, "It's my goal to make this finish as special for Jeanne as it is for me because this entire adventure has always been, and is now, a family thing not just my thing." Giving her this new ring had even more meaning than when I gave her the first one because now our love is even deeper. The ring was a Masterpiece Diamond with three stones that represent our past love, present love and future love.

Time: 4:23:00

We would have liked to have stayed and savored the moment longer, but Lake Placid was about to have a parade, and we needed to get out of town before the road closed. After a quick stretch that I dearly needed, we hastily hopped in the van and headed to our final destination of this trip, Niagara Falls. It was a six–hour drive from Lake Placid to Niagara Falls. We stayed at the Sheraton on the Canadian side. Since we were very low on funds, we did more walking around and sightseeing than going on actual activities. Austin and Erin did go on a ride called the Pile Driver, a tall mechanism that lifted its passengers several stories up in chairs and then dropped them. It was a ride promoted by World Wrestling Entertainment, which is something both of them have grown very fond of over the past year. I've always tried to remind them that wrestling is fake, and that when I was a kid it was real. Of course, I enjoy it as much as they do, but I would feel better about it if the WWE would clean up the sexual innuendo that goes on. If we had more money, we probably would have gone into one of the six different haunted houses there. Instead, we just imagined from the outside, saying what each of us thought might be inside.

Monday morning there was just one more thing to do before heading home. We purchased tickets for the Maid of the Mist. This was a boat ride that takes passengers very near both the American and Canadian falls. Jeanne had already done this as a kid, so she stayed behind with Popcorn. We were given souvenir bright blue raincoats that kept us from getting drenched from the mist coming off the falls. The boat was packed with tourists, and there was very little room to move around. Regardless, it was a neat experience watching the tremendous gush of water pour over our heads and thunder down below, splashing our faces. It was a wet, but fun, ending to our marathon visit to New York. The last thing I did before leaving the state was to make a phone call back to Chicago.

I told Jeanne it was to Carla, who Jeanne believed was checking up on our cats. I told Jeanne that Carla thought someone else had been in our home. Nine hours later, when we finally made it home, Jeanne and the kids discovered that someone had been in our home. Before leaving, I made arrangements for a contractor to redo our bathroom and install a new hot water heater. The contractor, Ken Tentler, did an excellent job. This really made coming back very special. We were now home from this marathon, home from the D.C. and 50 state marathons. I had actually done it. When I first ran, I thought one marathon was special. Now, my family and I have a treasure of experiences from all 50 states.

Epilogue
The 50–plus and Beyond…
June 24, 2005

"Where's the next marathon?" That's the question I'm most frequently asked by friends who have heard my stories over the years. I have many good reasons to continue. There are 15 states I did not break fours hours in. There are two states I did not run the full 26.2 miles within the boundaries (Nebraska and West Virginia). I never qualified for Boston with the time required for my age. I've been reminded numerous times that, although I have run in all 50 states, there are three members of my family who have never been to Louisiana. There are some great international destinations that are very enticing. One hundred seems like a nice round figure to strive for. The people in the running world are wonderful to be associated with. Theoretically, by continuing to run, I would maintain my good health. The list of why to continue running goes on and on. However, if one presumes this story is about achieving marathon goals, then the essence of **OUR** accomplishment is completely missed.

This story is about **OUR** entire family achieving this quest together. Without them, I would never have done it. First, I would not have survived if it were not for all of those essential contributions Jeanne made. She booked the hotels, rental cars and campgrounds. She helped the kids organize and pack their stuff. She arranged to have our home looked after while we were gone. She pulled up maps from the computer and was my navigator. But the most important contribution she made was intangible. She simply was a great friend to have…my best friend. Next, Austin and Erin gave this quest its true purpose. Every parent hopes their kids will be normal, and that they will some day make a smooth transition into society. It's our job as parents to be the best guides possible. I see my two kids as being the purest sense of normal or innocence there is. Unfortunately, it's their confounding naivety that makes them exceptionally vulnerable in the real world. Compounding the problem is the difficulty they have learning academically. Knowing these challenges we have, I hope that you, the reader, can now surmise that the marathons were only the framework on which to build a much greater endeavor, that of providing Austin and Erin with real–life experiences to better prepare them for what lies ahead. For they will enter a world which no one can yet imagine.

So, when I dwell on "What's next?", I'm not exactly ruling out marathons, although I really want to do something different. Perhaps I'll try long bike rides next. Austin would like to see China. Jeanne is ready for anything with me as long as she doesn't have to run. I think Erin loves the sightseeing, but is not crazy about waiting so long for me to finish a marathon. So we'll have to see what the crystal ball holds. As is evident, this story is not intended to inspire anyone to run a marathon. Of course, if it does, I would surely like to know about it. As for inspiring others to be in marathons, I couldn't even get Jeanne interested in running, although she made my running possible. If I could have scripted this story, I would have won at least one marathon, qualified for Boston, and run my final marathon *with* Jeanne. Of course, things turned out okay without a script. Our memories of these trips are precious gifts we gave each other, to be taken out and enjoyed on cold Chicago nights. If this story has any inspiration to it, I would hope it would be to treasure one's family, whatever group of people that includes. One thing you can be sure of: whatever it is I do next certainly will include my family, for they are my **gifts** that have **treasure** within.

* * * *